THOMAS PAINE

returns with

COMMON SENSE

Johnny Teague

THOMAS PAINE
returns with
COMMON SENSE

HISTRIA
PERSPECTIVES

Histria Perspectives

Las Vegas ◊ London ◊ New York ◊ Palm Beach

Published in the United States of America by
Histria Books
7181 N. Hualapai Way, Ste. 130-86
Las Vegas, NV 89166 U.S.A
HistriaBooks.com

Histria Perspectives is an imprint of Histria Books. Titles published under the imprints of Histria Books are distributed in the United States and Canada by Simon & Schuster and worldwide through Unified Book Distribution. We appreciate your support of copyright by purchasing an authorized edition of this book and for respecting intellectual property laws by not reproducing, scanning, or otherwise distributing any part of it by any means without permission. You are supporting authors and enabling Histria Books to continue publishing books for everyone.

Library of Congress Control Number: 2025944654

ISBN 978-1-59211-692-8 (softbound)
ISBN 978-1-59211-717-8 (eBook)

Contents

The Awakening

I cannot describe how I have felt the last several months. I have been away from this land a long, long time. Where have I been? I cannot disclose. It is not that I am forbidden, it is just too hard to describe in terms that citizens of this culture can grasp. Now that I have some understanding, I feel it is necessary to commit my thoughts to paper.

In two of my major writings, *The Rights of Man* and *The Age of Reason*, I provided sequels entitled *The Rights of Man, Part The Second* and *The Age of Reason, Part The Second*. Looking back, it is interesting that I saw fit to do additions to these two, but never considered doing a *Common Sense, Part The Second*. The occasion in which I am endeavoring to apply those truths of *Common Sense* to the conditions of today is strange to me. Another more talented in this culture would have done a better job, I am sure. Then again, that person would not be me, Thomas Paine. Another writer would not be able to provide commentary on the current situation using the lens of one who lived through the inception of this nation. So here I am.

As to the title of this pamphlet, the reader may remember that I grappled with the title of the first one. I had considered calling it *Plain Truth*, but my friend Dr. Benjamin Rush suggested I use the title *Common Sense*. His title was the best. For consistency, I thought of titling this writing, *Common Sense, Part The Second*. But after being off the scene for a couple of centuries, I have decided to aptly name these thoughts, *Thomas Paine Returns with Common Sense*.

I am privileged to have the assistance of a historian named Ms. Tanswell. She has taken time to educate me on the condition of our nation in 2026. It is hard for me to fathom that I am sitting on the porch of my cottage writing this. The whole world has changed dramatically. It has taken me over five months simply to take in what this free nation has been able to accomplish. It has taken that time and more to grasp how far this "advanced" nation has fallen. This will be the focus of my writing.

Before I begin the second part of my work, *Common Sense*, let me describe what it was like the day of my arrival. I awoke on the first of January 2025 as best I can calculate. When I sat up, I was on the bottom floor of my cottage in the feather bed, which I had placed in the corner of the main room facing the two front windows. This is the dwelling the state of New York gave me in 1784. I was grateful to receive this home with almost three hundred acres. After giving away all the proceeds from my famous pamphlet calling for Independence, I had little to show for my vocational efforts. It was heartening to see the appreciation of the nation I chose to call my own.

Back to what happened on that cold morning—I was alarmed to have been transported back to this home in what I found was the present day. I looked around the home. It was almost in the exact condition as when I left it in 1806. Why did I leave that year? Let us say it was a mutual decision to which this community and I had agreed. The circumstance of my exit? A bullet was fired through my window from an angry New Rochelle resident discontented with my writings against religion and former President George Washington. Looking back, I understand the anger of the would-be assassin. I would have preferred it if he had attacked me with a pen rather than a bullet. The pen has always been my weapon of choice. Many credited my pen as the instrument that brought about the death of the British Empire in North America.

When I rose from my bed near the fireplace a few months ago, I walked out on my porch to see a little rock-hedged creek beside my front yard. It has a beautiful rock bridge crossing over it. There are huge houses to the left of my home, and a very active street to the right. I was completely disoriented. There was a sound of rushing wind on the road. I was very surprised to see the oddest closed carriages racing by at exorbitant speeds. No horses were attached. I walked back to the yard. I looked at the cottage. It was, indeed, the remnants of mine. Some changes were noted, but no doubt, this was my cottage. Where it sat, though, greatly confused me. It is now located on the very bottom part of my farm. This was not where my house originally sat.

I walked up a hill that I recognized, trying to ignore all the houses. I came upon the actual spot where my cottage once rested. There is a giant white house there now taking my home's place. I thought of walking up and asking the resident to explain where I was and why I was here, but my own demeanor would most likely have caused the resident alarm. I decided to prayerfully sort through this as best I could on my own.

I returned to my house. I sat inside for a good while. It seemed as if I had entered a museum DEDICATED TO ME! I walked around outside again. To my surprise, up the hill near the busy street was a bronze bust of my head with some complimentary words below. I walked a little farther to see a marker with carving. It told a story of how my body was once buried on that spot. I found it amusing. I was in my body then, as I am now. I suppose it is appropriate my body is not buried in this place at the present. The Lord's Resurrection came to mind.

I walked back to the little creek below my house. I took a handful of the water to wipe my face, seeking to clear my head. I returned to the porch. I sat there for the remainder of the day. I was not hungry. I was not thirsty. I was enamored by the beautiful trees that surround this place. I could not get over the hundreds of houses standing where the fields once lay. People were everywhere, on my farm. They had clothing that was different, some with less clothing than I was accustomed to. I wondered if they knew I was their neighbor, or at least had been. Again, the bust up from this old house gave me comfort. Perhaps the hatred for me has subsided in this community.

I went to bed that evening late. I found it hard to sleep, but the questions of the day zapped my strength. As I arose the next morning, I was alarmed to hear a key being inserted into my door. I wondered if perhaps I had entered the house of someone in this day, the house that once was mine but was no more. If it was occupied, the family took great pains not to change anything.

I walked toward the door. I called out before the person entered. I did not want to startle whoever it was. I heard a woman scream. Obviously, my good intentions were useless. The lady called back to me, "Who are you? Why are you here? Don't you know this historic home is off limits to the public? Are you homeless?" Those were a lot of questions. She sounded panicked. She would not open the door. I could see her through the window next to my desk. She stepped off the porch back into the yard as if ready to make a mad dash.

I responded to the woman's questions with, "I know this is going to sound odd, but I am Thomas Paine, the owner of this home. I once lived here, but I suppose it has been a while. I did not know this was a historic home. I just knew it was my cottage before my neighbors made it clear I was not welcome anymore. Am I homeless? From the looks of this home, I do not believe that is the case."

I then asked the woman, "Who are you? Why are you here? Why do you have a key? And pardon this question, what year is it?" The lady answered hesitantly. I could tell she felt as unbelieving as I did. She said, "My name is Suzanne Tanswell. I am here because I am overseeing the renovations of this house. I am the chairperson of Museum Affairs for the Paine Cottage. And it is 2025."

We both were silent—me on the inside of my house, her on the outside. I offered a resolution, "How about I come outside? Let's sit on the porch in the two rocking chairs. I think we both have a lot of questions." We spent the next six hours visiting. I will not go any further into the exchange. I will leave the subject with the fact that Ms. Tanswell took the next five months of her spare time to show me around and educate me concerning the events since my departure. She was kind to obtain a modern wardrobe of clothes to avoid drawing attention to myself. I introduced myself to no one else. She told no one either. What we experienced had to have been Divine. Thankfully, as a woman of faith, she conceded the fact. We felt it best not to let anyone else know. Whatever purpose Providence had in this encounter; we would leave it to Him to decide how to make it known.

After two more months of processing, I am now ready to write. I feel my time is short. Ms. Tanswell has been patient, explaining what she calls modern technology. She is using it to transfer my written thoughts into her preferred mode of recording—a laptop. Because my English is as old as I am, she has been able, after much discussion, to put my words in a manner understandable for this century. In my first pass through this country, I was commended for making my thoughts on governmental philosophy understandable to the everyday man. Though I admired John Locke, his mode of explaining political theory was very complex. I chose then to place my own view of the subject on a lower shelf. I seek to do so again.

What I have seen in this nation has devastated me. I was disoriented in January when I awoke from my centuries' nap. I am more so now as I see how this republic has been upended. I am pressed to raise the alarm as to the danger that awaits this nation if a change of course is not taken promptly. As I thought it through, I decided the best mechanism to do so was to reintroduce common sense to the matter. What follows are the observations of why we have government, what the role of government should be, the history of autocratic abuses, and the necessary steps to save America from herself. I do not know if this nation or its government is ready for the shock it will take to fix this. Regardless, the trend must be reversed, or my generation's suffering will have been in vain. Below is my charge titled *Thomas Paine Returns with Common Sense.*

Introduction

What I wrote in 1776 concerning the British government:

*"Perhaps the sentiments contained in the following pages, are not YET sufficiently fashionable to procure them general favour; **a long habit of not thinking a thing WRONG, gives it a superficial appearance of being RIGHT,** and raises at first a formidable outcry in defense of **custom. But the tumult soon subsides. Time makes more converts than reason.**"*

What I see today in the United States government:

A long habit of not thinking a thing wrong will give the appearance that it is right, but time will show the truth. I will use the pronoun "we" often in this writing as I am still an American, though one from ages past. We have become deceived to believe that the government knows best for us. We are under the impression the government is more equipped to determine what we need and do not need, what we should have or not have, what we should do and not do, what we should say and not say. It is wrong to believe this. The government does not know more than the people and does not necessarily have the people's best interest in mind. The natural hedonism that is innate in every human being causes those who are in power to do what is in their own best interest first.

Instead of taking responsibility and thinking for ourselves, we surrender our choices to the ones we place over us. We may not realize it at first, but over time, we will see that those in government grow more wealthy and powerful, while we, the people, grow poorer and weaker. As time passes, we realize the truth, but often it is too late to correct by natural recourse.

What I wrote in 1776 concerning the British government:

*"**The cause of America is in a great measure the cause of all mankind.** Many circumstances hath, and will arise, which are not local, but universal, and through*

*which the principles of all Lovers of Mankind are affected, and in the Event of which, their Affections are interested. The laying a Country desolate with Fire and Sword, **declaring War against the natural rights of all Mankind**, and **extirpating the Defenders thereof from the Face of the Earth**, is the Concern of every Man to whom Nature hath given the Power of feeling; of which Class, regardless of Party Censure, is the* **AUTHOR**. *"*

What I see today in the United States' government:

The conflict of freedom and government today is not restricted to America. This is a problem men and women face throughout the whole world. There is a war by the government to take away the rights of the governed. Today, as in my day, anyone who objects to governmental abuses is to be rooted out and destroyed. This is the motive behind the cancel culture, the arrests of people who disagree, like the men in Florida objecting to the Ukraine war, or the people on the sixth of September who had the audacity to suggest that elections can be corrupted.

We are being told we have no right to question the government. Yet the origin of our government was to be of the people, for the people, and by the people. Jefferson said that when a government ceases to represent the people, there comes a time to remove that government. But now this beast we have created fights for its own existence, much like many fear Artificial Intelligence will fight for its own existence with computer rising against its programmer and maker.

This continent was self-governed for almost two hundred years before Britain began to abridge freedoms by its autocratic rule in the 1700s. Many of the Tory persuasion had the false impression that a civilized society can only exist if the commoners are led by some form of aristocracy. That was proven false before the British came. It has been proven false since America threw off its yoke. It saddens me that we would seek to take back on the yoke at this hour.

Of the Origin and Design of
Government in General

What I wrote in 1776 concerning the British government:

*"SOME writers have so confounded society with government, as to leave little or no distinction between them; whereas they are not only different but have different origins. **Society is produced by our wants, and government by our wickedness**; the former promotes our happiness POSITIVELY by uniting our affections, the latter NEGA-TIVELY by restraining our vices. The one encourages intercourse, the other creates distinctions. The first is a patron, the last a punisher.*

Society in every state is a blessing, but Government, even in its best state, is but a necessary evil; in its worst state an intolerable one: for when we suffer, or are exposed to the same miseries BY A GOVERNMENT, which we might expect in a country WITHOUT GOVERNMENT, our calamity is heightened by reflecting that we furnish the means by which we suffer. Government, like dress, is the badge of lost innocence; the palaces of kings are built upon the ruins of the bowers of paradise."

What I see today in the United States' government:

Society is produced by our wants. We gather to fulfill needs corporately for survival, for business, for trade, for companionship, for recreation, and for congregational worship. Because individuals carry unique gifts, the banding together brings more opportunities, conveniences, goods, services, technology, and a synergism of sorts. However, such gatherings result in conflicts and disorder. Government is established to bring order and settle disputes. It is from our wickedness that government is established. Just like in the beginning, Adam and Eve were naked and knew it not. Once they sinned, clothing was the cover, the ever-present

reminder that innocence had been lost. The existence of government is the reminder that we as a people cannot co-exist without some constraints.

What I wrote in 1776 concerning the British government:

*"For were the impulses of conscience clear, uniform and irresistibly obeyed, man
would need no other lawgiver; but that not being the case, he finds it necessary to
surrender up a part of his property to furnish means for the protection of the rest;
and this he is induced to do by the same prudence which in every other case advises him,
out of two evils to choose the least. Wherefore, security being the true design and end
of government, it unanswerably follows that whatever form thereof appears most
likely to ensure it to us, with the least expense and greatest benefit, is preferable to
all others."*

What I see today in the United States' government:

Because mankind's nature is selfish and not self-controlled, it becomes necessary to have a government mutually agreed upon to bring order and justice, while
having the ability to constrain and punish, to enforce the boundaries for each under its domain. This is necessary for the security of the individual and his possessions. To have such a protector, the individual must give up part of his rights to
determine for himself what he will do. He must also give up part of what he has
in order to provide for the government whose job it is to protect and secure the
rights, the life, and the assets of that individual.

At what cost is a society of individuals willing to pay for such protection? The
natural answer is as little as possible with the greatest benefit. There is a trade-
off—rights for protection, possessions for security. With any purchase, a person
determines how much of their savings they will give for the item desired. With
more benefits, one agrees to a higher price. There comes a point, however, that the
benefits offered are not worth the price required. Thus, the person settles for the
item with the bells and whistles within the limits they are willing to trade. It is the
same with government. We want the most benefits at the least cost, assuming that
we are the agents with the full authority to make that choice. There comes a point

today in this government where we are not given the choice. We are being governed against our consent. We are being required to give up more and more rights, gaining less freedoms for more governance against our consent.

The Chevron deference by the Supreme Court in 1984 gave the government the ability to do whatever, whenever it pleased under the guise of carrying out its duties on the advice of experts. This has resulted in an administrative state consisting of over four hundred agencies making demands on we the people without one consent recorded. I was horrified as I looked at what this government has devolved to be. I have observed infringements of a host of freedoms through actions by powered acronyms—EPA, FEC, FTC, FCC, ATF, FDA, DOJ, DOE, FBI, CIA, CDC, just to name a few. Most Americans do not know what these letters stand for, much less the freedoms they are taking day after day.

What I wrote in 1776 concerning the British government:

"In order to gain a clear and just idea of the design and end of government, let us suppose a small number of persons settled in some sequestered part of the earth, unconnected with the rest; they will then represent the first peopling of any country, or of the world. In this state of natural liberty, society will be their first thought. A thousand motives will excite them thereto; the strength of one man is so unequal to his wants, and his mind so unfitted for perpetual solitude, that he is soon obliged to seek assistance and relief of another, who in his turn requires the same. Four or five united would be able to raise a tolerable dwelling in the midst of a wilderness, but one man might labour out the common period of life without accomplishing any thing; when he had felled his timber he could not remove it, nor erect it after it was removed; hunger in the mean time would urge him to quit his work, and every different want would call him a different way. Disease, nay even misfortune, would be death; for, though neither might be mortal, yet either would disable him from living, and reduce him to a state in which he might rather be said to perish than to die.

Thus necessity, like a gravitating power, would soon form our newly arrived emigrants into society, the reciprocal blessings of which would supersede, and render the obligations of law and government unnecessary while they remained perfectly just to each other; but as nothing but Heaven is impregnable to vice, it will unavoidably happen that in proportion as they surmount the first difficulties of emigration, which bound them together in a common cause, they will begin to relax in their duty and attachment to each other: and this remissness will point out the necessity of establishing some form of government to supply the defect of moral virtue.

What I see today in the United States' government:

People band together for common needs. One man can only do so much. Two can be much more effective. Three, four, and five added to a common purpose become exponentially more efficient and effective, multiplying the impact they can make. Provided these grouped together are people of integrity who seek the best for everyone, there is no need for law or governance. All cooperate selflessly. In doing so, each benefits individually and in harmony. Sadly, on this side of Heaven, no person exists in that sublime state. People get lazy. They let others do the work. They get jealous. They lash out. They begin to store up for themselves. Distance grows. Society begins to disintegrate. There becomes a need for some form of governance or agreed-upon rules or law to supply the defect and lack of moral virtue.

What I wrote in 1776 concerning the British government:

Some convenient tree will afford them a State House, under the branches of which the whole Colony may assemble to deliberate on public matters. It is more than probable that their first laws will have the title only of Regulations and be enforced by no other penalty than public disesteem. In this first parliament every man by natural right will have a seat.

What I see today in the United States' government:

When such a society sees the problems, they gather to form rules by which all can abide, much like in a marriage or a business partnership. There is no punishment necessary; everyone participates in the rule-making and is convicted to follow. In sporting games, all agree to the rules: no holding, no going outside the lines, no getting a head start, and the like. A clean game is the request of all parties. In a marriage, both parties agree to the rules and adjustments made as conflict arises. All individuals have equal say in what those rules will be in the effort to live in harmony. Initially, the only enforcements necessary are personal conviction and the displeasure of the other parties. With moral truth on the inside of each person, governance is easily achieved. No punishment is required. This is what a society can have if they live together in close proximity, allowing dialogue concerning the rules of conduct, enforced by the common moral character.

What I wrote in 1776 concerning the British government:

*But as the Colony encreases, the public concerns will encrease likewise, and the distance at which the members may be separated, will render it too inconvenient for all of them to meet on every occasion as at first, when their number was small, their habitations near, and the public concerns few and trifling. This will point out the **convenience of their consenting to leave the legislative part to be managed by a select number chosen from the whole body, who are supposed to have the same concerns at stake which those have who appointed them, and who will act in the same manner as the whole body would act were they present.** If the colony continue encreasing, it will become necessary to augment the number of representatives, and that the interest of every part of the colony may be attended to, it will be found best to divide the whole into convenient parts, each part sending its proper number: and that the **ELECTED might never form to themselves an interest separate from the ELECTORS**, prudence will point out the propriety of having elections often: because as the **ELECTED might by that means return and mix again with the general body of the ELECTORS in a few months, their fidelity to the public will be secured by the prudent reflection of not making a rod for themselves. And as this frequent interchange will establish a common interest with every part of the community, they will mutually and naturally support each other,** and on this, (not on the unmeaning name of king,) depends the STRENGTH OF GOVERNMENT, AND THE HAPPINESS OF THE GOVERNED.*

What I see today in the United States' government:

As a society or colony of people increases, divisions and conflicts will continue to arise. Logistics make it impossible for all to come together to settle disputes and make new rules. Thus, each group will select a person to go in their place, to speak on their behalf, and to come to a settlement that is agreeable to all groups.

The problem foreseen long ago—if the representatives chosen, the Elected, do not frequently return to the group that sent them, they form their own group, drawing a line between the Elected versus the Electors. The Elected soon represent their own desires with no accountability. They sit in that governing body representing their own will and not the will of the people who sent them. There becomes a division. The Electors have given up their freedoms and their say to the ones they sent with no recourse. Thus, elections are necessary. Elections must be honest. Sadly, the Elected make the rules for the Elections, making it almost impossible to remove the ones who were sent, the ones who now seek to please the governing community they have since joined. The government gets stronger. The governed get weaker and less contented. It has always been my contention that one part of society should not be able to take away the rights of another. When the Elected are empowered and can remain a body in and of themselves with no dependence on the Electors, then one part of society can dictate to another. The Constitutional Republic is then lost.

What I wrote in 1776 concerning the British government:

Here then is the origin and rise of government; namely, a mode rendered necessary by the inability of moral virtue to govern the world; here too is the design and end of government, viz. Freedom and security. And however our eyes may be dazzled with show, or our ears deceived by sound; however prejudice may warp our wills, or interest darken our understanding, the simple voice of nature and reason will say, 'tis right.

What I see today in the United States' government:

As individual moral virtue fades, as internal governance is abandoned, the need for an external force, an outward governance, grows. Thus, we see the need for more and more laws. The codified command, "Thou shalt not steal" must be further clarified as morals lapse.

It is said some loggers in a remote part of America would cut their wood and then brand each to ensure payment for the work they had performed. Before long, some greedy or lazy workers would arise in the middle of the night, cut the end of other's logs and remark with their own brand. It was clear that this was stealing, but they declared it was not stealing but rather rebranding, which was not explicitly forbidden in the law. The result was that a new law had to be added to the theft law. It stated, "Thou shalt not cut the end of thy brother's logs and rebrand them with thine own mark."

The loggers continued their theft. Their excuse – they were not my brother's logs, so I am not violating the law. The law had to again be reworded, "Thou shalt not cut the end off anyone else's logs and rebrand them with thine own mark". The more we move away from internal virtue, the more our nature and reason say there is a need for governance. More laws are required to specify what a person should and should not do, though each knows in his heart what he is doing is either right or wrong. That point is clear when the one cutting and rebranding logs complains as his logs are rebranded.

What I wrote in 1776 concerning the British government:

I draw my idea of the form of government from a principle in nature which no art can overturn, viz. that the more simple any thing is, the less liable it is to be disordered, and the easier repaired when disordered; and with this maxim in view I offer a few remarks on the so much boasted constitution of England. That it was noble for the dark and slavish times in which it was erected, is granted. When the world was overrun with tyranny the least remove therefrom was a glorious rescue. But that it is imperfect, subject to convulsions, and incapable of producing what it seems to promise is easily demonstrated.

What I see today in the United States' government:

How true—the less complex something is, the easier it is to repair. The simpler a government is, the easier it is to correct. Look at what the government has become—look at all the departments—none of which answer to the people. Look how government employment has grown as a percentage of our national population. Look at how the Elected cannot and will not control the behemoth they have created. Even when elected representatives come and go, the governmental abuse continues regardless of what party is in power. To this date, there are more government agents with the right to arrest and bear arms than there are United States Marines. Such agents and agencies currently operate with little to no Congressional or Elected oversight. They function in a complex manner of overreach against all consent.

The Ten Commandments are simple, yet they cover virtually every conceivable transgression. Our Constitution is simple. It is also hard to change or amend. This is because the simpler something is, the less need for repair, and the less opportunity to distort. That very Constitution was written with the main goal of limiting what the government can do. It is effective if upheld. It is useless if ignored.

What I wrote in 1776 concerning the British government:

Absolute governments, (tho' the disgrace of human nature) have this advantage with them, they are simple; if the people suffer, they know the head from which their suffering springs; know likewise the remedy; and are not bewildered by a variety of causes and cures. But the constitution of England is so exceedingly complex, that the nation may suffer for years together without being able to discover in which part the fault lies; some will say in one and some in another, and every political physician will advise a different medicine.

What I see today in the United States' government:

In a simple government, the governed know who to blame. It is simple and it is clear. In the case of a monarchy, the populace only has one to blame—the king. In the case of an executive branch only, the populace knows that every decision the government makes comes from one person, and thereby the suffering is laid at his or her feet.

But the more complex the government gets, with this branch and that branch, this agency and that department, the cause for suffering cannot be discerned, and the government entities can easily point blame at the other while pretending to side with the people, keeping the pitchforks at bay.

What I wrote in 1776 concerning the British government:

I know it is difficult to get over local or long standing prejudices, yet if we will suffer ourselves to examine the component parts of the English Constitution, we shall find them to be the base remains of two ancient tyrannies, compounded with some new Republican materials.

First. — The remains of Monarchical tyranny in the person of the King.

Secondly. — The remains of Aristocratical tyranny in the persons of the Peers.

Thirdly. — The new Republican materials, in the persons of the Commons, on whose virtue depends the freedom of England.

The two first, by being hereditary, are independent of the People; wherefore in a CONSTITUTIONAL SENSE they contribute nothing towards the freedom of the State.

To say that the constitution of England is an UNION of three powers, reciprocally CHECKING each other, is farcical; either the words have no meaning, or they are flat contradictions.

What I see today in the United States' government:

In our system of government, the Executive, the Legislative, and the Judicial branches have devolved to be eerily similar to the King, the House of Lords, and the House of Commons. The Executive has taken more and more power than the Constitution grants. Thus, a tyranny has developed. The President now judges. The President now spends. The President now decides what laws he or she will enforce, and what laws he or she will not enforce.

The Senate has become the Aristocracy. The wealthiest of the wealthy hold those positions, and many times the positions are passed on to the next family member in succession, or to the person the current Senator chooses to replace him or her. The money to elect is then transferred to the favored successor, leaving little room for opposition to challenge. All the while surrendering its oversight to Executive agencies.

The House of Representatives stands as the House of Commons, being the Legislative unit closest to the people. But sadly, the virtue of that body has become as elitist as its partner. Against the Constitution, this half has surrendered its control of the purse to Executive orders.

The Supreme Court is to judge without regard to party or politics, based only on the letter of the Law as dictated in the Constitution. Each office holder pledges to uphold the Constitution, then each looks for ways to justify their actions through distorting the Constitution or deeming it as some outdated document. Virtue and simplicity are the strengths of that Constitution. Its truths are timeless. When the Constitution needs rectifying, which is rare, there is a method to do so. Sadly, we see our government leaders modifying it by fiat.

All three branches have become a society to themselves, doing what is best for their own group, neglecting the people who sent them. Those who run, run for the benefits to be in the select group rather than the virtue of standing for what is right and good for the constituents who selected them. The checks and balances of the three branches have become farcical. Together in cooperation, they now form the check on the freedoms and liberty of the people.

What I wrote in 1776 concerning the British government:

First. — That the King it not to be trusted without being looked after; or in other words, that a thirst for absolute power is the natural disease of monarchy.

Secondly. — That the Commons, by being appointed for that purpose, are either wiser or more worthy of confidence than the Crown.

But as the same constitution which gives the Commons a power to check the King by withholding the supplies, gives afterwards the King a power to check the Commons, by empowering him to reject their other bills; it again supposes that the King is wiser than those whom it has already supposed to be wiser than him. A mere absurdity!

There is something exceedingly ridiculous in the composition of Monarchy; it first excludes a man from the means of information, yet empowers him to act in cases where the highest judgment is required. The state of a king shuts him from the World, yet the business of a king requires him to know it thoroughly; wherefore the different parts, by unnaturally opposing and destroying each other, prove the whole character to be absurd and useless.

What I see today in the United States' government:

Our government has come to the point to believe that the President and the Congress are wiser than the people they govern. This is absurd, foolish, arrogant, and untrue. It is exceedingly ridiculous for any government authority to assume knowledge of all things. People in government who have never owned a business feel equipped to set laws limiting business. Government authorities who have never had to cover a payroll determine the tax rate based on the false premise that a business's profits are excessive. In some utopian sense, there is a belief that business should never make profits from which come investments and improvements. Governmental thought is that businesses exist to enrich the public, including the government officials, at a price-equal-cost rate. Agencies set regulations that hamstring enterprise, production, and agriculture. Claiming the public good, they damage both the public and the private. This is clearly seen in the recent drug shortages, resulting in the rationing of medicines to the citizens of this nation.

Today in America, the Executive, who has never had experience in the energy industry, seeks to regulate power plants by executive order. There is a power shortage for our citizens as a result. The Executive, through Central Planning, is forcing cargo ships to reach a point of zero emissions while penalizing them for emissions emitted until that is done. The consequence of government acting without knowledge has resulted in a decline in shipping, thus a shortage of goods. It is ridiculous that what the king of England did out of ignorance so long ago is being mimicked over two hundred years later in this government. These actions are destroying private enterprise, which will in turn reduce the resources to govern. Every resident will suffer in return.

There is a thirst for power inherent to all who can seize some. It is why monarchs seek to grow their kingdoms. They are not content to be the leader of a certain people, they then want to be the leader of more people. Ultimately, their desire is to be the ruler of all people. Even then, that thirst is not satisfied until they achieve the ultimate thirst for worship, being the object of all petitions, the giver of all needs. I cannot help but believe this is the root of the Climate Change policies of this nation. It is not enough to rule the people. The quest has reached the point of declaring government God, able to create life, terminate life, hold back the seas, and regulate temperature. It is absurd. Yet no one seems to take notice.

What I wrote in 1776 concerning the British government:

Some writers have explained the English constitution thus: the King, say they, is one, the people another; the Peers are a house in behalf of the King, the commons in behalf of the people; but this hath all the distinctions of a house divided against itself; and though the expressions be pleasantly arranged, yet when examined they appear idle and ambiguous; and it will always happen, that the nicest construction that words are capable of, when applied to the description of something which either cannot exist, or is too incomprehensible to be within the compass of description, will be words of sound only, and though they may amuse the ear, they cannot inform the mind: for this explanation includes a previous question, viz. **HOW CAME THE KING BY A POWER WHICH THE PEOPLE ARE AFRAID TO TRUST, AND ALWAYS OBLIGED TO CHECK?** *Such a power could not be the gift of a wise people, neither can any* **power, WHICH NEEDS CHECKING, be from God***; yet the provision which the constitution makes supposes such a power to exist.*

What I see today in the United States' government:

How did the President gain the power for which the people are afraid to trust, and more simply fear? A government of the people should never be one that is feared by the people. The opposite should be the case; the government of the people should fear the people and answer to them. Sadly, we the people fear our government and have little recourse to correct it.

What I have observed these months back in this nation is a government with free rein that refuses to answer constituents' questions. Constituents call, write, and email (a blessed tool) their elected officials with concerns. They are answered with form letters, nothing more. The Elected officials say they are doing the work of the people, and yet the people have no say in what they do. We look at the School Board meetings where parents are called terrorists for objecting to the way the education of their children has been removed from their purview. I have attended several City Council meetings of late. The Electors, our friends and neighbors, appear before the Council to voice concerns or complaints. The Electors are given one to three minutes to state their case. The Elected choose a rule of order in which they disallow themselves to give a response or an answer. The voter is then to step away from the microphone, somehow contented that they had the privilege to speak to their officials. What good is it to speak if one is not heard! That is today's government.

The beginning of wisdom is to fear God. Repeatedly, we hear our Elected say, "So help me God," and then demand God has no role in the subject. This government has no fear of God, no fear of judgment, no fear of war, no fear of repercussions, and no fear of consequences. The thing that is not thought wrong will continue to be considered right, but time will show the foolishness of such. God was the One referenced throughout the formation of this government and nation. Now God is the One who is chiefly prohibited from its practice.

What I wrote in 1776 concerning the British government:

*But the provision is unequal to the task; the means either cannot or will not accomplish the end, and the whole affair is a Felo de se: for as the greater weight will always carry up the less, and as all the wheels of a machine are put in motion by one, **it only remains to know which power in the constitution has the most weight, for that will govern**: and tho' the others, or a part of them, may clog, or, as the phrase is, check the rapidity of its motion, yet so long as they cannot stop it, their endeavours will be ineffectual: The first moving power will at last have its way, and what it wants in speed is supplied by time.*

What I see today in the United States' government:

The part of government that has the most weight will govern. That weight has been given more to the Executive branch agencies that govern apart from the people. It has the advantage of time, which the other parts of government do not.

People die. Agencies do not. There must be a control placed on agencies. There must also be a sunset for such.

What I wrote in 1776 concerning the British government:

*That **the crown is this overbearing part in the English constitution** needs not be mentioned, and that **it derives its whole consequence merely from being the giver of places and pensions is self-evident**; wherefore, though we have been wise enough to shut and lock a door against absolute Monarchy, we at the same time have been foolish enough to put the Crown in possession of the key.*

What I see today in the United States' government:

The Executive and Legislative branches derive their power from their ability to give place and pension, position, and money. It is the very means by which every candidate now campaigns—a promise of what he or she will give upon election. The voting public blindly follows, holding out the vote to the one who vows to give more. To appease the most at the detriment of the whole, the current rulers of this nation promise pay without work, lower lending rates for not paying debt, citizenship for those who refuse to apply, free tuition to those who will not pay, retirement for those who neglect to save.

Before long, the majority of our people meet at the fountain of government welfare. Who then is left to save America? In the Revolutionary War, General Washington, exasperated, asked, "Are these the men I must defend America with?" The same can be asked of this generation. As the nation and our freedoms are sinking into disrepair, are there any men and women who will defend us and keep us free?

On my walk through a neighborhood in New Rochelle, I met a young mother with whom I have become acquainted recently. Her daughter with her was crying. I asked what was wrong with the poor lass. The mother let me know that her daughter was being picked on in school. I asked the young girl if she had any friends at school. She replied she had just one. I encouraged her to rejoice in the one, ignore the rest. I told her the greatest travesty would be to give in to the crowd to ease the mocking. Often, standing brings the ire of the masses, but in the end brings honor above all. I call to any person in office who has a hint of virtue left to do the same. Stand for this nation, separate from the graft. Do what is best for all, even when it means persuading each person to fend for themselves without government assistance. Our nation can rise again with such a resolve.

What I wrote in 1776 concerning the British government:

*The prejudice of Englishmen, in favour of their own government, by King, Lords and Commons, arises as much or more from national pride than reason. Individuals are undoubtedly safer in England than in some other countries: but **the will of the king is as much the law of the land** in Britain as in France, with this difference, that **instead of proceeding directly from his mouth, it is handed to the people under the formidable shape of an act of parliament**. For the fate of Charles the First hath only made kings more subtle—not more just.*

What I see today in the United States' government:

Instead of having three separate branches, our government now lets the Executive dictate his plan. The Congress goes about doing what it can to accomplish its goals. Many of the laws the Legislative branch passes come from the will of the Executive with little pushback. What is more, executive agencies issue mandates directly to the public, bypassing a Congress more interested in luxury than in representing the people who sent them. Another example I revisit time and again in this writing, the Executive's ability to spend money without it being appropriated in Congress. No wonder this nation is $40 trillion in debt. I am a mathematician by hobby, yet even I cannot comprehend such an amount.

What I wrote in 1776 concerning the British government:

Wherefore, laying aside all national pride and prejudice in favour of modes and forms, the plain truth is that IT IS WHOLLY OWING TO THE CONSTITUTION OF THE PEOPLE, AND NOT TO THE CONSTITUTION OF THE GOVERNMENT that the crown is not as oppressive in England as in Turkey.

An inquiry into the CONSTITUTIONAL ERRORS in the English form of government, is at this time highly necessary; for as we are never in a proper condition of doing justice to others, while we continue under the influence of some leading partiality, so neither are we capable of doing it to ourselves while we remain fettered by any obstinate prejudice. And as a man who is attached to a prostitute is unfitted to choose or judge of a wife, so any prepossession in favour of a rotten constitution of government will disable us from discerning a good one.

Of Monarchy and Hereditary Succession

What I wrote in 1776 concerning the British government:

MANKIND being originally equals in the order of creation, the equality could only be destroyed by some subsequent circumstance: the distinctions of rich and poor may in a great measure be accounted for, and that without having recourse to the harsh ill-sounding names of oppression and avarice. Oppression is often the CONSEQUENCE, but seldom or never the MEANS of riches; and tho' avarice will preserve a man from being necessitously poor, it generally makes him too timorous to be wealthy.

*But there is another and great distinction for which no truly natural or religious reason can be assigned, and that is the **distinction of men into KINGS and SUBJECTS. Male and female are the distinctions of nature, good and bad the distinctions of Heaven; but how a race of men came into the world so exalted above the rest, and distinguished like some new species, is worth inquiring into,** and whether they are the means of happiness or of misery to mankind.*

What I see today in the United States' government:

All men and women were created equal. There were no distinctions at our creation, nor at our birth. There are distinctions of nature—male and female. There are distinctions by God—good and bad. There are distinctions of chance and effort—rich and poor. But how did the distinction of kings and subjects come about? I will comment on that below.

I wish to take time to deal with an issue that has greatly disturbed me this second time around on this earth. Nature and Nature's God have made the distinction of male and female. I am a man of science. I am a man of reason. I have always believed that in nature, we see all the attributes and intentions of God. There have been many opinions on nearly everything under the sun, but never have I known a differing opinion as to who was male and who was female.

As I have watched your culture, read the news, and observed the protests, I am confounded that the most basic of truths is now distorted. Men claim to be women. Women claim to be men. Men claim to ovulate. Women claim to father children. No science says a man can become a woman. Let a man ask himself, "Where is the research that says gender modification is healthy for children?" The European nations tried this. They are leaving this insanity because they have found it destructive. Yet this nation is embracing the lie. Men competing against women defies anatomical certainties. The outcomes reaffirm the science. Men are stronger than women. Men are faster than women. Men are equipped for the physical rigors of battle. Women have children. Women have gifts that no man could ever acquire, despite his desire. Science, truth, and common sense object to what is happening in this age.

What about common decency? Early in our existence as a nation, children were abused in sweatshops. They were forced to do things that neither their body nor minds could tolerate. A great move was made to protect the children, to support their innocence, to provide a moral foundation upon which they could build their lives. Today, children are treated as objects of desire. Men can shower with girls. Women can use the restroom with boys. Men are allowed to prey on minors—male and female. Your television and movie productions are promoting such depravity as virtuous. Your children's program, Sesame Street, and the corporation Disney promote the most unnatural fetishes. These are mental manipulators. With God and good parenting, these can be offset. But then the government allows the educational institution to trump parental authority. The declaration that children do not belong to the parents but to society has enabled the assault.

What's worse? The physical modification by the medical society to sterilize our American youth. We outlawed children from working until a certain age. We prohibited them from drinking or smoking until they reached a year of maturity. We deemed their judgment inadequate to vote until the age of eighteen. Yet, we are allowing eight-year-olds to have their sex changed on the whim of an unstable parent or an abusive teacher? In one of our northern states, the government is allowing children to be taken from parents who object to their genital mutilation. Again, I am a man of science; the DNA is clear. Nature and Nature's God have deemed who is male and who is female. Let a man ask, "Can we make the sun set in the East? Can we reverse the rotation of the Earth?" The answer is no. The same answer comes to the question of gender. It cannot be changed regardless of what surgical arts are applied.

What I wrote in 1776 concerning the British government:

*In the early ages of the world, according to **the scripture chronology** there were no kings; the consequence of which was, there were no wars; it is the pride of kings which throws mankind into confusion. Holland, without a king hath enjoyed more peace for this last century than any of the monarchical governments in Europe. Antiquity favours the same remark; for the quiet and rural lives of the first Patriarchs have a snappy something in them, which vanishes when we come to the **history of Jewish royalty**.*

*Government by kings was first introduced into the world by the Heathens, from whom the **children of Israel** copied the custom. It was the most prosperous invention **the Devil** ever set on foot for the promotion of idolatry. **The Heathens paid divine honours to their deceased kings, and the Christian World hath improved on the plan by doing the same to their living ones. How impious is the title of sacred Majesty applied to a worm, who in the midst of his splendor is crumbling into dust!***

As the exalting one man so greatly above the rest cannot be justified on the equal rights of nature, so neither can it be defended on the authority of scripture; for the will of the Almighty as declared by Gideon, and the prophet Samuel, expressly disapproves of government by Kings.

What I see today in the United States' government:

The Scripture chronology displays a truth—when there were no kings but God, there were no wars. When the position of king was accepted, pride led to war and confusion. It was the godless who first established the position of king. It was the people of God, the Jewish people, who sought to be like everyone else. They suffered the results. When our government is that of man and not of God, this is the natural progression, be it a monarch, a dictator, a democracy, or a republic.

The heathen then began to deify their dead kings. We deify our living rulers. We give them our subjection, our trust. We surrender our freedoms to their will. We fool ourselves into believing their actions are in our best interest. We reverence mere mortals who have the same intellect and the same pace of decay in their mortal bodies as we have in ours.

Exalting a group of men or a man above all others defies nature. It violates equal rights for all, a level base on which we all abide, whether we recognize it or not. It is a grave offense against our Creator God.

I wish to correct myself from my blasphemous writing entitled *The Age of Reason*. After months in a French prison, feeling betrayed, growing sick and delusional, I lashed out against God, against America, and even against President George Washington. At first, I questioned Scripture. Then I sought to discredit it. I mocked the mysteries, the miracles, and the prophecies. I contended that the New Testament was mythology, that the Old Testament was a distortion of God, and that the Jewish leaders were murderers. I ended life a bitter man. Yet in my heresies, at my death, I sought to be buried as a Quaker, though I knew they would object. They refused me burial in their sacred ground. Let the reader know that all misconceptions end at death. Upon graduation from this life, each person will stand before God. The lies fall away. Truth is all one sees. I began my life correctly, standing on God's Word. A good beginning does not guarantee a good ending. I ended badly. I can write today that God's Word, the Bible, is true. There is not an error in one jot or tittle.

Let the reader also know, apart from coming face-to-face with God, the evidence is clear with the finding of the Dead Sea Scrolls. God's Word has not changed, been manipulated, or corrupted by ambitious Church leaders. Even the crooked King James could not successfully bring falsehood to the Word of God, no more than Balaam could pronounce a curse on the Jewish people. The prophecies of the Text written long ago were carried into complete fulfilment. The locations and dates are reliable. Archaeological findings are proving the people referenced did exist, the events did occur.

The life of Jesus was not recorded centuries after He lived as I once penned. They were written by eyewitnesses who amassed the words and works of this One from God committing them to paper for the salvation of the world. I once questioned the miracles yet believed in life after death. If a dead man has not been raised, then how can any dead have hope. The empty tomb in Jerusalem declares that Jesus did come, that He did live, that He did work miracles which culminated

in His perfect life being sacrificed for the sins of others, placing the emphatic ex-
clamation with the greatest of all miracles—His own resurrection.

As I read my own *Common Sense*, I value how I walked with God then. As I
think of my sad *Age of Reason*, I see how far the mighty can fall. I ask forgiveness
for my past rebellion. I rejoice in the opportunity to set the record straight. My
peers were right to disown a self-loving, caustic old man. As the reader reads this
writing and sees the conflict with my past heretical benediction to the life first
lived, let he or she know I have been corrected by the Almighty. Let the record
show.

What I wrote in 1776 concerning the British government:

*All anti-monarchical parts of scripture have been very smoothly glossed over in
monarchical governments*, but they undoubtedly merit the attention of countries
which have their governments yet to form. *"Render unto Cesar the things which are
Cesar's" is the scripture doctrine of courts*, yet it is no support of monarchical government, *for the Jews at that time were without a king, and in a state of vassalage to
the Romans.*

*Near three thousand years passed away, from the Mosaic account of the crea-
tion, till the Jews under a national delusion requested a king. Till then their form
of government* (except in extraordinary cases where the Almighty interposed) *was a
kind of Republic, administered by a judge and the elders of the tribes. Kings they
had none, and it was held sinful to acknowledge any being under that title but the
Lord of Hosts. And when a man seriously reflects on the idolatrous homage which
is paid to the persons of kings, he need not wonder that the Almighty, ever jealous
of his honour, should disapprove a form of government which so impiously invades
the prerogative of Heaven.*

What I see today in the United States' government:

When the Lord Jesus said, "Render to Caesar what is Caesar's and to God what
is God's", the Jewish people were vassals, slaves to the Roman empire. For three
thousand years, Israel had no king, but more of a republic ruled by judges and the
elders of the tribes. To have a king or to make government our king is an offense

to the Lord of Hosts. He makes no allowance for homage to be given to any man in the person of a king, or a President, or a member of Congress, or a Supreme Court Justice. This invades the prerogative of Heaven. God dictates what is good and bad. He is the only One who does not disintegrate like a worm, who does not become forgetful, tired, or weak. His judgments do not waver. He does not err. His Scripture, His Precepts, His Laws were incorporated into our Constitution and form of self-government. This "one nation under God" is how we have flourished and prospered in peace. Leaving Him is how we have devolved and grown adversarial in word and deed.

The French Revolution was evidence of what a nation can become when it throws out God. The French Revolution is also a sign of our future if we continue this destructive path. I suffered under it firsthand. The Church was attacked, as were all clergy. Antichristian dogma dominated. I once greased its wheels. The French leadership under the Jacobins felt all authority was evil, even the Authority of God. Was the nation better? NO! People of religion were being killed at the altar of the guillotine. Mobs ran amok, slaughtering the innocent and the guilty alike.

I grieve that while I was in a prison condemning God, the self-acclaimed god Robespierre ran roughshod over all that is good. Was the French nation better for rejecting God? Let the countless mass graves from that day answer. It was in these burial places, the French disposed of thousands of people. They gutted people, cut off hands and feet, severed heads to place on poles, parading their trophies in the streets. People took advantage of the mobs to rid themselves of adversaries by labeling them enemies of the state. There were no trials, just beheadings at one of the numerous guillotines. We are seeing the state of the United States government do the same. It goes unchecked because it acts in the cloak of secrecy enabled by an adoring press.

The French Revolution denounced God as king. They removed King Louis XVI as king. They vowed no king. Then they made Robespierre their king. Soon after, they elevated Napoleon. What Nietzsche wrote is true. When a nation banishes God, there is a vacuum to fill. People will worship another god. They will make another king. That king will be self, science, sex, nature, pleasure, a man, a woman, a President, a school of thought, or an idea, but there will be a king. There will be a god. I choose God to be my King. It was my desire for this nation in *Common Sense* the first go-round. It is my longing today.

What I wrote in 1776 concerning the British government:

Monarchy is ranked in scripture as one of the sins of the Jews, *for which a curse in reserve is denounced against them. The history of that transaction is worth attending to.*

The children of Israel being oppressed by the Midianites, Gideon marched against them with a small army, and victory thro' the divine interposition decided in his favour. The Jews, elate with success, and attributing it to the generalship of Gideon, proposed making him a king, saying, "Rule thou over us, thou and thy son, and thy son's son." Here was temptation in its fullest extent; not a kingdom only, but an hereditary one; but Gideon in the piety of his soul replied, "I will not rule over you, neither shall my son rule over you. THE LORD SHALL RULE OVER YOU." Words need not be more explicit: Gideon doth not decline the honour, but denieth their right to give it; neither doth he compliment them with invented declarations of his thanks, but in the positive style of a prophet charges them with disaffection to their proper Sovereign, the King of Heaven.

What I see today in the United States' government:

God delivered Israel from a nation that had a king. He did so by a man who was not worthy to be a king or a general or to have any success. God made the difference with Gideon. Israel, with God and no king, defeated a nation without God but with a king. It made no sense then that they should want to have a king and not God. They were choosing to be like the ones they defeated. How are we like that in our nation? Communism was falling. Capitalism was succeeding. Then when the USSR fell, we decided to be like them? Our society has surpassed all others; now we want to be like the other nations? That will only bring us down in defeat.

Gideon had success. The people wanted to make him king. General George Washington had success. The people wanted to make him king. We praise God that Gideon knew who gave the victory. He declared there is no king but God! He was a man of piety and reverence for God, with no desire to take credit for what God had done. The same for General George Washington after his success, he gave all glory to God, refusing to be made a king. Ah that we would have such virtue today—where men and women realize God is the Giver of all good things, that He alone should be praised, and that we each will stand before Him in judgment. We should live with that reality and that fear which will guide our steps to virtue.

Gideon said, as the people clamored to make him their king, it is not their right to make anyone king over them. God is their king, He alone. But today, we have pushed out God. We have decided we will make the kings and follow men and women in government leadership instead of God. We have done so at a great cost. The government said close the churches, the schools, the businesses. We quickly obliged. Government said wear masks and get a vaccination. We took that as a command to be followed, not questioned. A doctor lost his license for speaking against the mandates. The nation sits silently. We surrendered our rights, which are unalienable, God-given. These rights are not to be revoked by the government. They are not to be surrendered by the citizens. God has given them. He alone can remove them.

What I wrote in 1776 concerning the British government:

*About one hundred and thirty years after this, they fell again into the same error. The hankering which the Jews had for the idolatrous customs of the Heathens, is something exceedingly unaccountable; but so it was, that laying hold of the misconduct of Samuel's two sons, who were intrusted with some secular concerns, they came in an abrupt and clamorous manner to Samuel, saying, "Behold thou art old, and they sons walk not in thy ways, now make us a king to judge us like all the other nations." And here we cannot observe but that their motives were bad, viz. that **they might be LIKE unto other nations**, i. e. the Heathens, whereas **their true glory lay in being as much UNLIKE them as possible**. "But the thing displeased Samuel when they said, give us a King to judge us; and Samuel prayed unto the Lord, and the Lord said unto Samuel, hearken unto the voice of the people in all that they say unto thee, **for they have not rejected thee, but they have rejected me, THAT I SHOULD NOT REIGN OVER THEM**. According to all the works which* *they have done since the day that **I brought them up out of Egypt even unto this day, wherewith they have forsaken me, and served other Gods**: so do they also unto thee. Now therefore hearken unto their voice, howbeit, protest solemnly unto them and show them the manner of the King that shall reign over them," i.e. not of any particular King, but the general manner of the Kings of the earth whom Israel was so eagerly copying after. And notwithstanding the great distance of time and difference of manners, the character is still in fashion. "And Samuel told all the words of the Lord unto the people, that asked of him a King. And he said, **This shall be the manner of the King that shall reign over you. He will take your sons and appoint them for himself for his chariots and to be his horsemen, and some shall run before his chariots"** (this description agrees with the present mode of impressing men) **"and he will appoint him captains over thousands and captains over fifties, will set them to clear his ground and to reap his harvest, and to make his instruments of war, and instruments of his chariots, And he will take your daughters to be confectionaries, and to be cooks, and to be bakers"** (this describes the expense and luxury as well as the oppression of Kings) **"and he will take your fields and your vineyards, and your olive yards, even the best of them, and give them to his servants. And he will take the tenth of your seed, and of your vineyards, and give them to his officers and to his servants"** (by which we see that bribery, corruption, and favouritism, are the standing vices of Kings) **"and he will take the tenth of your men servants, and your maid servants, and your goodliest young men, and your asses, and put them to his work: and he will take the tenth of your sheep, and ye shall be his servants, and ye shall cry out in that day because of your king which ye shell have chosen, AND THE LORD WILL NOT HEAR YOU IN THAT DAY."** This accounts for the continuation of Monarchy; neither do the characters of the few good kings which have lived since, either sanctify the title, or blot out the sinfulness of the origin; **the high encomium of David takes no notice of him OFFICIALLY AS A KING, but only as a MAN after God's own heart.** "Nevertheless the people refused to obey the voice of Samuel, and they said, Nay, but we will have a king over us, that we may be like all the nations, and that our king may judge us, and go out before us and fight our battles." Samuel continued to reason with them but to no purpose; he set before them their ingratitude, but all would not avail; and seeing them fully bent on their folly, **he cried out, "I will call unto the Lord, and he shall send thunder and rain"** (which was then a punishment, being in the time of wheat harvest) **"that ye may perceive and*** *see that your wickedness is great which ye have done in the sight of the Lord, IN ASKING YOU A KING. So Samuel called unto the Lord, and the Lord sent thunder and rain that day, and all the people greatly feared the Lord and Samuel. And all the people said unto Samuel, Pray for thy servants unto the Lord thy God that we die not, for WE HAVE ADDED UNTO OUR SINS THIS EVIL, TO ASK A KING."* These portions of scripture are direct and positive. They admit of no equivocal construction. That **the Almighty hath here entered his protest against monarchical government is true,** or the scripture is false. **And a man hath good reason to believe that there is as much of kingcraft as priestcraft in withholding the scripture from the public in popish countries. For monarchy in every instance is the popery of government.**

What I see today in the United States' government:

I am referencing Scripture again to argue against a king, a monarchy, or a government that dictates and governs against the will of the people. I am reemphasizing a truth I stated so clearly over two hundred years previous—it is wrong for a king or a priest to withhold Scripture from the public! It is wrong for the government to do that or for any religion to do the same. When a case comes before the Supreme Court of our land, the Constitution is referenced for chief guidance in the decision. When a law is considered in Congress, the Constitution is cited to substantiate the legality or illegality of the act. When a President gives an order, the Constitution is checked to see if he indeed has that authority. The Constitution is the law of the land. I am citing a greater law in *Common Sense*. The Holy Scripture of God is the highest law of this land, nay the whole world. It is immutable. It is inerrant. The Constitution has set forth ways for it to be modified or amended. God has given no such path regarding His Word. Why? God's Word needs no amending.

To make one's argument solid, the Holy Scripture provides the final word on all issues of life. There was no better way to lay out the argument for the American Revolution than referring to God's Word. There is no better way to lay out a new start for this American Government than referring to God's Word. The enemies of this nation have sought to remove this reference, cutting the chain to the anchor that holds it steady. They have sought to cast aside God's Word, ripping the foundation under which this nation was built. There should be no surprise now that it is crumbling.

When the nation of Israel cried out for a king, God, speaking through the prophet Samuel, let them know emphatically what an autocratic form of government would do to them. He said it will take their children and use them for its own good. It will make war, sacrificing their sons and daughters with little care for the hurt it brings to their families. It will treat every citizen as a mere pawn to use how they see fit. It will enslave the people to serve for whatever luxuries it desires for itself. It will take individuals' fields, homes, businesses, assets for whatever pleasures or punishments it defines necessary. Beyond that, it will take taxes at its discretion and increase them as it sees fit to meet its excessive spending. In a word, the autocratic government empowered by the people will become a monster that cannot be contained, turning on its leash against the owner that fed it.

Currently, this government has spent $40 trillion more than it has gathered. To levy taxes to a degree to offset spending would bring a government overthrow. So instead, the government borrows. It borrows without check. It spends even more than it can borrow. As a result, it prints paper money to cover its bills. At some point, that paper will have no value. A collapse is soon coming. No business, no industry, no nation can spend more than it has for long. We are being told that the government must pay its debts. That sounds right. It is right. A government should pay its debts. But a government also should not spend more than its revenue. A government should borrow no more than what it can pay back. All common sense says, "Stop spending. Stop borrowing. Get your house in order. This nation is going to fail." Yet not one takes a stand. Each year, every year, at the fiscal cliff, the debt ceiling is raised. The autocratic government gives itself a license to spend and borrow more. Let this paragraph serve as the epitaph when the burial of a great nation is completed.

Regarding an absconding government, recently a ninety-four-year-old woman was unable to pay the $12,000 she owed on her property taxes. The government seized her home. It sold her home at a huge profit, keeping the proceeds. In essence, the government did just as God foretold. It took the woman's home for its own desires. Common sense would dictate, at worst, the sale of the home to recoup the $12,000 in arrears, and then the return of the proceeds from the home to the lady so that she might have something on which to live. We have left the wisdom we have been given, forfeiting individual rights to the federal authorities.

It is interesting, God noted that when the nation of Israel sinned against God, they lost the production of their fields. That came through a storm, through the weather that God sent. We are being told the climate is getting hotter. That is not necessarily true. So now they say the climate is becoming erratic. It has always been erratic. But let the reader ask, if the climate is changing, if natural disasters are increasing, could not the cause be rejection of God rather than emission of carbon?

Israel wanted to be like other nations. That was a problem. Israel was never to be like any other nation. America was never to be like any other nation either. We, like ancient Israel, are to be like the nation God created us to be—founded on His Word, a nation of the people, for the people, and by the people.

What I wrote in 1776 concerning the British government:

To the evil of monarchy we have added that of hereditary succession; and as the first is a degradation and lessening of ourselves, so the second, claimed as a matter of right, is an insult and imposition on posterity. **For all men being originally equals, no one by birth could have a right to set up his own family in perpetual preference to all others for ever, and tho' himself might deserve some decent degree of honours of his contemporaries, yet his descendants might be far too unworthy to inherit them.** *One of the strongest natural proofs of the folly of hereditary right in Kings, is that nature disapproves it, otherwise she would not so frequently turn it into ridicule, by giving mankind an ASS FOR A LION.*

What I see today in the United States' government:

All men are equals, there is no one by birth who gains a higher position or a greater power. Though some leader may have done a good job for their people, this does not mean that their son or daughter will be equally gifted to do the same. A person may have earned honor for how he has served, but their offspring may be unworthy of such a position and completely incompetent to lead.

No person should have the ability to use government to set up their own family in perpetual preference to others. The free market allows prosperity for any who are willing to produce. Government is a service. Yet it has been used to enrich men and women of both political parties. We have seen office holders elected belonging to a certain tax bracket move to exponentially higher levels by merely being in office. This is beyond reason, other than corruption and greed.

Members of Congress saw that First Republic Bank was going to collapse. Knowing this before it became public knowledge, ahead of the market, members sold their shares in this bank making profits, avoiding losses because of the position of trust they had been given. This would be called insider trading for anyone else. The very Congress that profited put one of your celebrities, Martha Stewart, in jail for the same act. Such hypocrisy! How can the public let their officials set up their own families above the nation of families? How is it, after all of our suffering, to establish this nation, our nation lets its leaders live above the law? I donated the proceeds of my first *Common Sense* to help our nation's war effort. General Washington served without pay many times. James Madison had to leave Congress to make money at his estate because he was going broke serving his nation. Today, the opposite is true. This must change. Common sense demands it.

What I wrote in 1776 concerning the British government:

*Secondly, as no man at first could possess any other public honors than were bestowed upon him, so the givers of those honors could have no power to give away the right of posterity, and **though they might say "We choose you for our head," they could not without manifest injustice to their children say "that your children and your children's children shall reign over ours forever." Because such an unwise, unjust, unnatural compact might (perhaps) in the next succession put them under the government of a rogue or a fool.** Most wise men in their private sentiments have ever treated hereditary right with contempt; yet it is one of those evils which when once established is not easily removed: many submit from fear, others from superstition, and the more powerful part shares with the king the plunder of the rest.*

What I see today in the United States' government:

For years, our nation has disavowed heredity in leadership, especially when it comes to monarchy or a dictatorial government. Sadly, we have easily fallen back into this. At first, it was from John Adams to John Quincy Adams. Thankfully, John Quincy Adams earned the right by his own intellect, talents, service, and virtue. But today, we want a Clinton, or an Obama, or a Bush, or a Kennedy, believing that somehow those from leadership breed natural leaders. History shows the opposite is true. How dare we decide that those who rule over us shall have their children rule over ours. This nation should never have a ruling class.

What I wrote in 1776 concerning the British government:

*This is **supposing the present race of kings in the world to have had an honorable origin: whereas it is more than probable, that, could we take off the dark covering of antiquity and trace them to their first rise, we should find the first of them nothing better than the principal ruffian of some restless gang, whose savage manners of pre-eminence in subtilty obtained him the title of chief among plunderers; and who by increasing in power and extending his depredations, overawed the quiet and defenseless to purchase their safety by frequent contributions.** Yet his electors could have no idea of giving hereditary right to his descendants, because such a perpetual exclusion of themselves was incompatible with the free and restrained principles they professed to live by. Wherefore, hereditary succession in the early ages of monarchy could not take place as a matter of claim, but as something casual or complemental; but as few or no records were extant in those days, the traditionary history stuff'd with fables, it was very easy, after the lapse of a few generations, to trump up some superstitious tale conveniently timed, Mahomet-like, to cram hereditary right down the throats of the vulgar. Perhaps the disorders which threatened, or seemed to threaten, on the decease of a leader and the choice of a new one (for elections among ruffians could not be very orderly) induced many at first to favour hereditary pretensions; by which means it happened, as it hath happened since, that what at first was submitted to as a convenience was afterwards claimed as a right.*

What I see today in the United States' government:

We want to believe that whoever is in power reached that level of leadership through honorable means. Ashamedly, if we dare, we pull the curtain back to find many in power today obtained that position like some ruffian, gang member, or bully. They then revise history to cover the truth of their origin with a created flowery story. We fall into the assumption that those in office remain there because of their selfless performance, just to find that they retain their office because of the money they give out and the favors they promise.

What I wrote in 1776 concerning the British government:

England since the conquest hath known some few good monarchs, but groaned beneath a much larger number of bad ones: yet no man in his senses can say that their claim under William the Conqueror is a very honourable one. **A French bastard landing with an armed Banditti and establishing himself king of England against the consent of the natives, is in plain terms a very paltry rascally original. It certainly hath no divinity in it.** *However it is needless to spend much time in exposing the folly of hereditary right; if there are any so weak as to believe it, let them promiscuously worship the Ass and the Lion, and welcome. I shall neither copy their humility, nor disturb their devotion.*

What I see today in the United States' government:

William the Conqueror was considered an honorable king. Looking through the fog of deception, I realized he came to power with the help of armed bandits against the consent of the people. What we see in our nation today are "representatives" who have come to power using deception, cheating, and coercion. They govern for themselves, against the will of the people. The people have no remedy, especially if elections are not audited, monitored, and ensured to be honestly executed.

What I wrote in 1776 concerning the British government:

Yet I should be glad to ask how they suppose kings came at first? The question admits but of three answers, viz. **either by lot, by election, or by usurpation.** *If the first king was taken by lot, it establishes a precedent for the next, which excludes hereditary succession.* **Saul was by lot,** *yet the succession was not hereditary, neither does it appear from that transaction that there was any intention it ever should.* **If the first** *king of any country was by election, that likewise establishes a precedent for the next; for to say, that the right of all future generations is taken away, by the act of the first electors, in their choice not only of a king but of a family of kings for ever, hath no parallel in or out of scripture but the doctrine of original sin, which supposes the free will of all men lost in Adam; and from such comparison, and it will admit of no other, hereditary succession can derive no glory. for as in Adam all sinned, and as in the first electors all men obeyed; as in the one all mankind were subjected to Satan, and in the other to sovereignty; as our innocence was lost in the first, and our authority in the last; and as both disable us from re-assuming some former state and privilege, it unanswerably follows that original sin and hereditary succession are parallels. Dishonourable rank! inglorious connection! yet the most subtle sophist cannot produce a juster simile.*

What I see today in the United States government:

How are rulers chosen? By lot, by election, or by usurpation? In Israel, the first king was chosen through lot—Saul. Could it be that by that first lot, all kings to follow were chosen through his offspring? God intervened.

If a nation elects a man President, let's say John F. Kennedy or George H.W. Bush, does that then mean that one election determined that all successors come from the Kennedy or Bush line? If that is the case, then the generations to follow that first election have no say in who their next leader will be. The implication is that the first choice of our parents becomes our required choice thereafter. This follows the hereditary pattern we have been stuck with through man's whole existence. Adam sinned, so all sin. We choose one, so all must follow the same. God forbid. He has intervened countless times in this nation. May He continue to do so. He gave the rights to the Electors. The Electors do not have the right to give those rights away.

What I wrote in 1776 concerning the British government:

As to usurpation, no man will be so hardy as to defend it; and that William the Conqueror was an usurper is a fact not to be contradicted. The plain truth is, that the antiquity of English monarchy will not bear looking into.

*But it is not so much **the absurdity as the evil of hereditary succession which** concerns mankind. Did it ensure a race of good and wise men it would have the seal of divine authority, but as it opens a door to the FOOLISH, the WICKED, and the IMPROPER, it hath in it the nature of oppression. Men who look upon themselves born to reign, and others to obey, soon grow insolent. Selected from the rest of mankind, their minds are early poisoned by importance; and the world they act in differs so materially from the world at large, that they have but little opportunity of knowing its true interests, and when they succeed in the government are frequently the most ignorant and unfit of any throughout the dominions.*

What I see today in the United States' government:

If hereditary acquisition of power bred only good and wise men, it would have God's Hand in it. Sadly, we get foolish, wicked, and improper leaders this way. Under hereditary acquisition, men and women begin to look at themselves as born to lead, while all others are born to follow. This is where we are today when we have no term limits. Wealth is accumulated while in office, to pass down the name, the money, and the donors to their privileged offspring or selected successors.

The shame about this is, many in office today have had only one profession, one vocation to draw from their entire lives—governing. They have no experience, no exposure to the real world, work, needs, or interests of the people. Such tunnel-visioned leaders must rely on lobbyists and government "experts" to guide their legislative ship. The result, rather than having the best in government to lead, we have more frequently been cursed with the most ignorant and unfit at every level of government. Those in office then parade in nakedness, stripping the nation bare, forcing others to glorify their bereft of achievements.

What I wrote in 1776 concerning the British government:

*Another evil which attends hereditary succession is, that the throne is subject to be possessed by a minor at any age; all which time the regency acting under the cover of a king have every opportunity and inducement to betray their trust. **The same national misfortune happens when a king worn out with age and infirmity enters the*** *last stage of human weakness. In both these cases the public becomes a prey to every miscreant who can tamper successfully with the follies either of age or infancy.*

What I see today in the United States' government:

This nation has bred a royal blood over its existence—the Adams, the Harrisons, the Tafts, the Roosevelts, the Rockefellers, the Kennedys, the Bushes. Digging deeper, we can see that many members of Congress come from family members who have prior held political office at some level—the Pelosis, the Huckabees, the Fords. When we allow hereditary succession to political office, we get people who are too young and inexperienced. We also get hamstrung with people too old and infirm to wisely guide a nation. Let the voter beware of this habit.

What I wrote in 1776 concerning the British government:

The most plausible plea which hath ever been offered in favor of hereditary succession is, that it preserves a nation from civil wars; and were this true, it would be weighty; whereas it is the most bare-faced falsity ever imposed upon mankind. The whole history of England disowns the fact. Thirty kings and two minors have reigned in that distracted kingdom since the conquest, in which time there has been (including the revolution) no less than eight civil wars and nineteen Rebellions. Wherefore instead of making for peace, it makes against it, and destroys the very foundation it seems to stand upon.

What I see today in the United States' government:

There is a belief that if we let those in power remain in power, that if we grow our central government, then we will not be affected by the back-and-forth mechanizations of elections and parties. Some have even suggested suspending elections entirely. They say this will end all divisions, but history rejects that notion. The more the ruling powers separate from those governed, the greater the need to fortify the governing from the threats and objections of the governed.

What I wrote in 1776 concerning the British government:

*The contest for monarchy and succession, between the houses of York and Lancaster, laid England in a scene of blood for many years. Twelve pitched battles besides skirmishes and sieges were fought between Henry and Edward. Twice was Henry prisoner to Edward, who in his turn was prisoner to Henry. And so uncertain is the fate of war and the temper of a nation, when nothing but personal matters are the ground of a quarrel, that Henry was taken in triumph from a prison to a palace, and Edward obliged to fly from a palace to a foreign land; yet, as sudden transitions of temper are seldom lasting, Henry in his turn was driven from the throne, and Edward re-called to succeed him. **The parliament always following the strongest side.***

What I see today in the United States' government:

Instead of standing for the people, and standing even more for what is right, the parliament and sadly Congress stand with the side that is strongest and/or richest. The little guy has no one to defend his property. The unknown mother sits in the open garage of her home, weeping over the inability to get anything done for her handicapped daughter. The elderly lady writes letters to her Congresswoman every week for help with her husband's Social Security mess-up. She receives a form letter. Nothing more. This was to be a government of the people, for the people, by the people. Hear the words of the writer of Proverbs: "*Wisdom calls aloud in the street, she raises her voice in the public squares; at the head of the noisy streets, she cries out, in the gateways of the city she makes her speech*" and "*Does not wisdom cry out? Does not understanding raise her voice? On the heights along the way, where the paths meet, she takes her stand; beside the gates leading into the city, at the entrances, she cries aloud.*" Common sense cries out the same. Yet, no one will listen.

What I wrote in 1776 concerning the British government:

This contest began in the reign of Henry the Sixth, and was not entirely extinguished till Henry the Seventh, in whom the families were united. Including a period of 67 years, viz. from 1422 to 1489.

In short, monarchy and succession have laid (not this or that kingdom only) but the world in blood and ashes. 'Tis a form of government which the word of God bears testimony against, and blood will attend it.

If we enquire into the business of a King, we shall find that in some countries they may have none; and after sauntering away their lives without pleasure to themselves or advantage to the nation, withdraw from the scene, and leave their successors to tread the same idle round. In absolute monarchies the whole weight of business civil and military lies on the King; the children of Israel in their request for a king urged this plea, "that he may judge us, and go out before us and fight our battles." But in countries where he is neither a Judge nor a General, as in England, a man would be puzzled to know what IS his business.

What I see today in the United States' government:

In absolute monarchies, the whole weight of business, civil, and military lies with the king. Sadly, the whole weight of business, in private and in public, along with the military and policing, lies now under the feet of the federal government. This current autocracy has broken the veil between public and private enterprise. Now government (including the President by Executive order) acts as an absolute monarch, dictating what businesses will operate (clean energy), what product will be sold (electric vehicles), what business type (coal) will be shuttered.

What I wrote in 1776 concerning the British government:

The nearer any government approaches to a Republic, the less business there is for a King. It is somewhat difficult to find a proper name for the government of England. Sir William Meredith calls it a Republic; but in its present state it is unworthy of the name, because the corrupt influence of the Crown, by having all the places in its disposal, hath so effectually swallowed up the power, and eaten out the virtue of the House of Commons (the Republican part in the constitution) that the government of England is nearly as monarchical as that of France or Spain. Men fall out with names without understanding them. For 'tis the Republican and not the Monarchical part of the Constitution of England which Englishmen glory in, viz. the liberty of choosing an House of Commons from out of their own body—and it is easy to see that **when Republican virtues fail, slavery ensues. Why is the constitution of England sickly, but because monarchy hath poisoned the Republic; the Crown hath engrossed the Commons.**

What I see today in the United States' government:

The nearer a government gets to being a Republic, the less business there is for a king. The reason the U.S. Congress has so many bills (thousands of pages in each), dealing in every area of life, is because this government is no longer functioning as a Republic but rather as a distorted oligarchy. This government has swallowed up power in every area of this nation. It has ceased to be an entity elected by the people. The government in Washington, D.C. now selects whom it chooses to be the representatives of the people through endorsements, media connections, and financial support. Thus, this government is as dictatorial as Britain was, as France was, as Spain was, as China and Russia are. When Republican virtues (not the party but the form of government) are discarded, slavery ensues. This is the state of America. The Constitution is no longer enforced, nor is there adherence to it. The Republic has been poisoned.

Look at the laws that are passed. Let the reader ask, "How many of these laws are further restricting the citizens? Are the laws limiting government or growing government?" Dr. Ben Franklin was asked in 1787 in Philadelphia as he walked out of Independence Hall, "What have we got, a republic or a monarchy?" Dr. Franklin was prescient in his reply, "A republic if you can keep it." I grieve when I observe that, as things now stand, the Republic has been lost. A monarchy style of government has imprisoned the Republic.

It was the corrupt influence of the crown that ruined the Republic of Britain. It is the corrupt influence of power that has caused those in authority to separate from the people, forming an alliance against we the people. The government has extended its tenacles to the smallest of matters. It has threatened to remove Medicare and Medicaid funding if a candle in a hospital sanctuary in Tulsa, Oklahoma is not removed. Its intrusion includes the toilets we flush, the lightbulbs we burn, the cars we drive, the surgeries we can have, the nails we can use, the labels we should place on our products, the disclaimers we must run with our commercials, and more. The Republic has been lost at worst. At best, it is on life support attended by federal hospice volunteers.

What I wrote in 1776 concerning the British government:

In England a King hath little more to do than to make war and give away places; which, in plain terms, is to empoverish the nation and set it together by the ears. A pretty business indeed for a man to be allowed eight hundred thousand sterling a year for, and worshipped into the bargain! Of more worth is one honest man to society, and in the sight of God, than all the crowned ruffians that ever lived.

What I see today in the United States' government:

The President, like the King, makes war, gives away places, allows illegal immigrants in while giving them money that Americans earn, spending more money than the nation brings in, bankrupting this nation.

In Michigan, land is being given to a foreign business of a communist country, an enemy of this nation. Farmers living in that area, who dare speak against such villainy, face daily threats of losing their own land as a result. This is not a republic. This is not a nation governed by the people. This is a land governed by usurpers. Our residents are slaves who must adhere to the dictates of a ruling class.

Thoughts on the Present State
of American Affairs

What I wrote in 1776 concerning the British government:

IN the following pages I offer nothing more than simple facts, plain arguments, and common sense: and have no other preliminaries to settle with the reader, than that he will divest himself of prejudice and prepossession, and suffer his reason and his feelings to determine for themselves that he will put on, or rather that he will not put off, the true character of a man, and generously enlarge his views beyond the present day.

What I see today in the United States' government:

The purpose of this writing is to provide simple facts laced with common sense so that the readers can enlarge their views and determine for themselves what is right and what is wrong in government. Perhaps this generation has been so mistaught that what goes on in this nation is considered the way it was supposed to be. This may be the reason why I have been allowed to speak to you. A voice from the past, a cry of our Founders who have risen to awaken this generation before it is too late—to say NO this was not why we fought, bled, and died. We suffered to give our posterity freedom and liberty. Our offspring have squandered it away, but for what? Prosperity? Peace?

There is a cry for reparations for those who were once enslaved. That has a familiar ring. My compatriots and I suffered under the rule of Britain. We were treated as slaves. We worked for them. Our product was claimed by their ownership. We fought for our own freedom. What were our reparations then? It was freedom. That was our payment. That is what we sought. All those who have been emancipated on this continent have been rewarded with the precious gift of liberty.

They have the right to self-determination, to face obstacles and overcome them. This is what freedom is. Let me tell the reader what freedom is not. Freedom does not depend on the government for a handout or a pay-back. A nation where the people are free is a nation where individuals become what their will and intellect aspire to.

Governor Patrick Henry asked my generation a question. I will ask it of you, "Is life so dear, or peace so sweet, as to be purchased at the price of chains and slavery?" Please let the reader pause to consider this. Mr. Henry's answer was the one my friends agreed to, "Forbid it, Almighty God! I know not what course others may take; but as for me, give me liberty or give me death!" Please wake up. Please take back the Republic. Take back your government, people.

What I wrote in 1776 concerning the British government:

*Volumes have been written on the subject of the struggle between England and America. Men of all ranks have embarked in the controversy, from different motives, and with various designs; but all have been ineffectual, and **the period of debate is closed. Arms as the last resource decide the contest; the appeal was the choice of the King, and the Continent has accepted the challenge.***

What I see today in the United States' government:

The die is cast. The lines have been drawn. A fight for self-government has once again been thrust upon this citizenry. You must accept the challenge. We erected a government where the people could take a stand for themselves. We armed our citizens to combat government abuses. Yet, the call in this nation's streets is to take the guns from the Americans.

A marine was on one of your underground trains in New York. A man there who had been arrested previously over forty times was threatening the passengers with bodily harm. A soldier came to his neighbors' rescue. He held the assailant in a chokehold, not to kill but to restrain him. Now that courageous one is being considered a murderer for defending his fellow citizens? What was better? Let the assailant kill a few passengers? Has this nation lost its mind?

What I wrote in 1776 concerning the British government:

*It hath been reported of **the late Mr. Pelham** (who tho' an able minister was not without his faults) that on his being attacked in the House of Commons on the score that his measures were only of a temporary kind, replied, "THEY WILL LAST MY TIME." Should a thought so fatal and unmanly possess the Colonies in the present contest, the name of ancestors will be remembered by future generations with detestation.*

The Sun never shined on a cause of greater worth. 'Tis not the affair of a City, a County, a Province, or a Kingdom; but of a Continent — of at least one-eighth part of the habitable Globe. 'Tis not the concern of a day, a year, or an age; posterity are virtually involved in the contest, and will be more or less affected even to the end of time, by the proceedings now. Now is the seed-time of Continental union, faith and honour. The least fracture now will be like a name engraved with the point of a pin on the tender rind of a young oak; the wound would enlarge with the tree, and posterity read in it full grown characters.

What I see today in the United States' government:

What we are up against, some will say is only temporary, that the rights of the people will swing back to their favor over time. Most do not worry about the abuses of government at this moment. The belief continues that with a new administration, or at the next election, things will return to a safer state. That return is in jeopardy if no counter is made. Now is the seed time to push back, to pull the weeds that are crowding out the fruitful plants. If we do not stop these abuses now, they will not go away; they will grow more intrusive with each passing year. The result will be enslavement of the masses to the villainy of the few.

I rejoice to read of a school board member in California who took a stand for science when he pushed against the transgender indoctrination in the schools. His school board quickly removed him from his seat. They held a special election to fill the vacancy. The exiled school board member ran again for his seat. He chose to let the people decide who should represent them, not the governing board. The Electors chose him, the one removed, to be reseated to do the work of the people.

If only the national citizenry would do the same. This government would be readily corrected.

I rejoiced that in Texas, there were state legislators who realized how great this nation has fallen from its values. They understood the strong foundation this nation sits upon is not the Constitution first, but God's Law. As a result, these Texas legislators moved to have the Ten Commandments restored in every classroom. I grieve that at the last moment, they were defeated. When will we understand that the Great Law Giver is the only King we should have? If He governs our hearts, we will need little government outside that confine. I make a promise today. The mass shootings in this nation will decline steadily with each tablet of commandments restored in a classroom. Your schools will be safer, as will your marketplace. The boardroom will be honest, as will your state house. Return to the God of this nation. Return to the Republic created under God's watchful care.

What I wrote in 1776 concerning the British government:

*By referring the matter from argument to arms, a new era for politics is struck—a new method of thinking hath arisen. **All plans, proposals, &c. prior** to the nineteenth of April, i.e. to the commencement of hostilities, **are like the almanacks of the last year; which tho' proper then, are superseded and useless now.** Whatever was advanced by the advocates on either side of the question then, terminated in one and the same point, viz. a union with Great Britain; the only difference between the parties was the method of effecting it; the one proposing force, the other friendship; but it hath so far happened that the first hath failed, and the second hath withdrawn her influence.*

What I see today in the United States' government:

The remedies of a trespassing government are quickly being removed, and soon will be like last year's almanacs. They were useful in that year, but no longer have any utility now. If we do not take a stand now, our Constitution and our elections will be pleasant memories from a past day unrecoverable. The old saying, "You don't know what you have until it is gone," applies to lost love, lost time, lost possessions, lost freedoms, and a lost nation. Do not let what was created for our good be lost.

What I wrote in 1776 concerning the British government:

As much hath been said of the advantages of reconciliation, which, like an agreeable dream, hath passed away and left us as we were, it is but right that **we should examine** *the contrary side of the argument, and enquire into some of* **the many material injuries which these Colonies sustain, and always will sustain, by being connected with and dependent on Great Britain. To examine that connection and dependence, on the principles of nature and common sense, to see what we have to trust to, if separated, and what we are to expect, if dependent.***

I have heard it asserted by some, that as America has flourished under her former connection with Great Britain, the same connection is necessary towards her future happiness, and will always have the same effect. Nothing can be more fallacious than this kind of argument. We may as well assert that because a child has thrived upon milk, that it is never to have meat, or that the first twenty years of our lives is to become a precedent for the next twenty. But even this is admitting more than is true; for I **answer roundly that America would have flourished as much, and probably much more, had no European power taken any notice of her.** *The commerce by which she hath enriched herself are the necessaries of life, and will always have a market while eating is the custom of Europe.*

What I see today in the United States' government:

As the colonist came to this continent to be free, a dependence developed upon Great Britain for resources, for protection, and for a customer of goods. Such a reliance went from one voluntary to one mandatory. Dependence was the object of the government of England. She chose to determine how we would live, what we would raise, where we would sell, what we would buy, who we would sell to, what we would pay, and the taxes that would be levied. Today's American government has taken Great Britain's place. The American government has encouraged greater reliance upon it for resources. It has extended itself to be the chief consumer of goods grown or produced. This current government, which is growing without bounds, mandates dependence—how we will live, what we will sell, what we will buy, who we will sell to, what we will pay, and the taxes that will be levied. We have become vassals through the empowering of those who rule over us. The

Elected who rule would have no authority had it not been surrendered apathetically by the Electors.

Think of how the government has subsidized industry. Think of how the ruling "elite" has determined how we will graze cattle, the specifications for manufacturing, the restrictions of resources, the blocking of certain businesses from borrowing, and the decision to force some industries to die on the vine. The rulers' reach has expanded down to a ridiculous dictate of what material is to be used in manufacturing drinking straws. Every person doing work while living in this nation must cast an eye on the agencies in charge to see if their approval has been gained. Our populace has been relegated to the position of a child seeking a parent's permission. That role was reversed in my day. It needs to be reversed back to the founding.

What I wrote in 1776 concerning the British government:

But she has protected us, say some. That she hath engrossed us is true, and defended the Continent at our expense as well as her own, is admitted; and she would have defended Turkey from the same motive, viz.—for the sake of trade and dominion.

Alas! we have been long led away by ancient prejudices and made large sacrifices to superstition. We have boasted the protection of Great Britain, without considering, that her motive was INTEREST not ATTACHMENT; and that she did not protect us from OUR ENEMIES on OUR ACCOUNT; but from HER ENEMIES on HER OWN ACCOUNT, from those who had no quarrel with us on any OTHER ACCOUNT, and who will always be our enemies on the SAME ACCOUNT. Let Britain waive her pretensions to the Continent, or the Continent throw off the dependence, and we should be at peace with France and Spain, were they at war with Britain. The miseries of Hanover last war ought to warn us against connections.

What I see today in the United States' government:

We run to the protection of this government. We cede more and more freedom in exchange for the government's protection. The primary reason the government protects us is for its own endurance and profit. We have lazily allowed the government to provide for our security—from enemies, from health crises, and for retirement needs. By doing so, we give up our guns, trusting the government will fight for us. We worry not about our health, believing the government will care for us when we are sick. We have ceased to save money with the reliance that the government will meet our needs when we become old or disabled. All the while, we are exchanging precious freedoms to the whims of those in government who promise to meet our needs. We have exchanged the big "G" God for the little "g" government. All of us are poorer for it.

This form of governance was created with three basic responsibilities—to protect our Life, our Liberty, and our Pursuit of Happiness. Instead, this government takes life, paying for abortions and euthanasia. Instead, it is taking liberty day by day. This government covers its actions with the excuse that it is doing what it is to ensure the happiness of the citizens. It deludes itself into thinking that if the citizens own nothing, they will be happy. The rulers of this nation have not become the exception but the co-conspirator with the ruling bodies of the world. "They know best" is their mantra. Through unlimited submission, we have allowed the government to drag us before it to demand answers from we the people. We stand before our government as if before Almighty God. We come before them, praying that God will give us favor before the government. Again, it is the government that was intended to be dragged before us to answer for its actions. IT IS TO ANSWER TO US, NOT THE OTHER WAY AROUND! Can you hear me?

What I wrote in 1776 concerning the British government:

It hath lately been asserted in parliament, that the Colonies have no relation to each other but through the Parent Country, i.e. that Pennsylvania and the Jerseys and so on for the rest, are sister Colonies by the way of England; this is certainly a very roundabout way of proving relationship, but it is the nearest and only true way of proving enmity (or enemyship, if I may so call it.) France and Spain never were, nor perhaps ever will be, our enemies as AMERICANS, but as our being the SUBJECTS OF GREAT BRITAIN.

What I see today in the United States' government:

Family relations are being destroyed, claiming that no one is a family to them-selves, but rather the collective, the village, the community is the only relation that matters. As our current Administration has said, "There is not such a thing as someone else's child. They are all our children, our nation's children." The focus is on the collective, and that collective is found only under the government's care. This makes it easy for our children to be taught things contrary to their parents' wishes. The custody of the children has been transferred to the state. It is legal then for the government to oversee a sex change or an abortion by a minor. That child is now seen as belonging to the government alone to raise and decide. The parent has one requirement—provide housing for the state's youth. Is it not enough that this generation of Americans has given up their freedoms? Are they now to give up their children? Hear me again. If you give up your freedoms, your land, your self-responsibility, and your children, your life will soon be required.

What I wrote in 1776 concerning the British government:

*But Britain is the parent country, say some. Then the more shame upon her conduct. Even brutes do not devour their young, nor savages make war upon their families. Wherefore, the assertion, if true, turns to her reproach; but it happens not to be true, or only partly so, and the phrase **PARENT OR MOTHER COUNTRY** hath been jesuitically adopted by the King and his parasites, with a low papistical design of gaining an unfair bias on the credulous weakness of our minds. Europe, and not England, is the parent country of America. **This new World hath been the asylum for the persecuted lovers of civil and religious liberty from EVERY PART of Europe. Hither have they fled, not from the tender embraces of the mother, but from the cruelty of the monster; and it is so far true of England, that the same tyranny which drove the first emigrants from home, pursues their descendants still.***

What I see today in the United States' government:

I wrote that Britain calls itself the parent country, yet she devoured her young. She made war upon her families. How much more is the American government doing the same? It interposes itself as the parent, free to kill babies and destroy families through a welfare program that increases dependence more. A wicked farmer can feed the chickens and water them. Later when the farmer, in cruelty, plucks the chicken of all its feathers, the wicked farmer laughs with glee as the chicken comes to nestle against the warmth of his legs. So is this government, which has moved far from what was intended.

This government makes no requirements on its youth but dependence. It mandates no red ink in grading, no failing in school, no correction of spelling. It calls mathematics a racial science. It revises history in the name of not hurting delicate feelings. It gives the same size trophies to those who fail as to those who succeed. It has weakened the minds of the vassals, making them weaker still. The slave holder in our nation (with whom I waged war upon my whole life) sought to keep the slaves from an education to prevent them from realizing chains could be discarded. This government gives degrees with no accomplishments, graduates the illiterate, promising a free education. A free education? Is it free because it has no worth? The people's oppressive governing body extends its provision to housing, phones, and food. The dependence upon it grows, but no one notices.

Many fled to this nation to escape the cruelty of the monster overseas, just to find the same tyranny exists on these shores. Where now can we flee if this nation is lost, if this government is not changed, if these lords are not removed?

What I wrote in 1776 concerning the British government:

In this extensive quarter of the globe, we forget the narrow limits of three hundred and sixty miles (the extent of England) and **carry our friendship on a larger scale; we claim brotherhood with every European Christian, and triumph in the generosity of the sentiment.**

What I see today in the United States' government:

I review what I wrote in 1776. I grieve that now this nation no longer claims a brotherhood with every European Christian nor has a friendly sentiment to the Christian religion. As the reader reviews my pamphlet, may all prejudices and historical revisionism be put aside. This nation was founded as a Christian nation with an ethic grounded in that sacred Text called the Bible. It was from that Text that we formed our laws and determined what is right and what is wrong. This was done because what God has given us through His Scripture is immutable. The rights we have were given by Him and are unalienable. They cannot be altered. Moving this nation away from that foundation has cut the rudder, letting the ship of this nation drift into treacherous waters with no control. She will not be able to survive. I call upon every reader to retrieve the rudder of God's Word before it is too late. My fear is that it may be too late.

Late in life, in my delusion, I concluded that the Bible was filled with evil actions by Jewish people under God's cruel orders. The Bible I once memorized became to me a collection of evil, manipulated distortions of the history of God. When I wrote *The Age of Reason,* I was sitting in a prison under the order of Robespierre during the French Revolution. I questioned how the Bible could order the killing of people groups whom God deemed wicked. While I wrote *The Age of Reason,* I relate back to hearing the screams of the pregnant women outside my prison bars being gutted with their children ripped from their wombs and smashed against the rock walls. I heard the screams of fathers as their children were beheaded before them. I saw justice removed; trials discarded. Execution was the order of Robespierre. In reflection, I wonder how better our world would have been had God ordered Robespierre killed at birth, or for that matter, Manasseh, Herod, Antiochus Epiphanes, Hitler, and Stalin? The killings prescribed by God, as recorded in Scripture, made sense. It was not cruel for Him to make such orders. It was mercy that He did. He can make those decisions, we cannot. I have lived a long time since the birth of this nation. I recant my delusions which I penned offending the wise God. His Word is true. It is, above all, beneficial that this nation was founded upon His Word. We must return to it if we seek life, liberty, and happiness.

What I wrote in 1776 concerning the British government:

It is pleasant to observe by what regular gradations we surmount the force of local prejudices, as we enlarge our acquaintance with the World. **A man born in any town in England divided into parishes, will naturally associate most with his fellow parishioners (because their interests in many cases will be common) and distinguish** *him by the name of NEIGHBOR; if he meet him but a few miles from home, he drops the narrow idea of a street, and salutes him by the name of TOWNSMAN; if he travel out of the county and meet him in any other, he forgets the minor divisions of street and town, and calls him COUNTRYMAN, i.e. COUNTYMAN; but if in their foreign excursions they should associate in France, or any other part of EUROPE, their local remembrance would be enlarged into that of ENGLISH-MEN.* And by a just parity of reasoning, **all Europeans meeting in America, or any other quarter of the globe, are COUNTRYMEN; for England, Holland, Germany, or Sweden,** when compared with the whole, stand in the same places on the larger scale, which the divisions of street, town, and county do on the smaller ones; Distinctions too limited for Continental minds. **Not one third of the inhabitants, even of this province, [Pennsylvania], are of English descent. Wherefore, I reprobate the phrase of Parent or Mother Country applied to England only, as being false, selfish, narrow and ungenerous.**

What I see today in the United States government:

This nation is losing its identity. Being an American is not valued. We have become African American, Irish-American, Franco-American, Mexican-American. Many have dropped "American" altogether. We are becoming a gathering of individuals—African, Irish, French, Mexican, with no concern for the durability of this nation. The concern devolves to that of individuals getting the most they can for themselves at the expense of all others. This is enhanced with the rejection of the Biblical ethic. There is no impetus to fight for the land in which we live. We have no allegiance. We are satisfied to live under whatever rule or ruler that comes, as long as we profit. The Holy Script describes this as the state of Israel during the time of the judges. The norm being everyone did what was right in their own eyes with no mooring to an ethical standard.

The flag of this nation is burned in disrespect. No one stands at its anthem. Others demand two anthems. History revised makes it seem that this precious nation was conceived through some crime. Let me attest, I was there. This nation was birthed against the crime of tyranny. Some say this nation was built on slavery. This is true in that Great Britain was a vicious master. We, as its slaves, built it. Others would object, saying no, this nation was built on African slavery. That is

revising history. Some of this nation's founders were slaveholders, no doubt. The
vast majority were not. We fought against our own to end it when I walked this
earth for the first time. We set the wheels in motion to eradicate this evil. We
established a method for its eventual extinction. Ultimately, we took arms against
each other to abolish it forever. Yet, it is a false reflection that has instilled hatred
for this Republic. This superior style of government is being replaced by an oppressive one, which will reinstitute slavery in a universal form.

The federal government does not enforce the borders. Thousands are coming
in illegally each day, bringing danger and harm, taking jobs and resources. These
who cross unlawfully have no desire to be Americans. They have no willingness to
become part of this nation's fabric. They are aliens taking up residence in an oblig-
ing land. The federal government gives a wink of approval, letting it happen. If
such a practice were held to a vote, Americans would vote to close the border immediately. Within the realm of common sense, no one leaves the front door to
their home open at all hours. Why are our officials doing that with our nation?
Britain forced their soldiers into our homes and towns. This government is forcing
illegal immigrants into ours. Further, when the borders are open, when all are
considered eligible for the provision from the citizen taxpayer, all allegiance falters.
Disorder ensues. Ultimately, destruction comes upon the free nation which was
dearly sacrificed for at its inception.

What I wrote in 1776 concerning the British government:

*But, admitting that we were all of English descent, what does it amount to?
Nothing. Britain, being now an open enemy, extinguishes every other name and
title: and to say that reconciliation is our duty, is truly farcical.* The first king of
England, of the present line (William the Conqueror) was a Frenchman, and half the
peers of England are descendants from the same country; wherefore, by the same method
of reasoning, England ought to be governed by France.

What I see today in the United States' government:

Let me for a moment reason with those who hate this nation for the wrong
reason. Let me contend with those who have brought about a move from the solid

foundation. Many have distanced this nation from being a Constitutional Republic in the quest for fairness. This government was formed to make all equal, to give all equal opportunity, not equal outcome. The pilgrims tried to have equal outcomes, where all shared what was raised in common. That did not work. Before long, people who refused to work ate the same amount of food as the people who did work. The people who worked grew tired of feeding those who would not help, so they reduced their efforts. The whole nearly starved to death. Then a change was made. Each was given private property. Each was responsible for their own provision and that of their families. It was only then that this nation began to thrive. Dependence upon God and self-responsibility produced the greatest nation on the face of the earth. Britain then came to take what we bountifully produced. Again, a reticence to produce followed. Dependence or rebellion were the choices. Rebellion won out.

Why all this? When a government begins to dictate, the people have choices—depend or rebel, acquiesce or resent. I rebelled then. I resent now the current trend. As to the choice of monarchy or republic, the recent generation has blindly decided it prefers a form of monarchy. Such an autocracy requires little thought on the part of the individual. I resent this. With all the blood that was spilt, including my own, this generation chooses willingly to be enslaved? For sure, the Elected are willing to be the masters with no end to their tenure, with no desire to limit their terms. But for the Electors to willingly bow the knee? I cannot relate to such an adversarial position on the rights of men.

What I wrote in 1776 concerning the British government:

Much hath been said of the united strength of Britain and the Colonies, that in conjunction they might bid defiance to the world. But this is mere presumption; the fate of war is uncertain, neither do the expressions mean anything; for this continent would never suffer itself to be drained of inhabitants, to support the British arms in either Asia, Africa, or Europe.

Besides, what have we to do with setting the world at defiance? Our plan is commerce, and that, well attended to, will secure us the peace and friendship of all Europe; because it is the interest of all Europe to have America a free port. Her trade will always be a protection, and her barrenness of gold and silver secure her from invaders.

What I see today in the United States' government:

I have seen, in this nation that I once knew, a hatred for commerce. Does the reader not see that it is commerce and trade that have secured peace and friendship with the world? It has been the ingenuity of this free people that has vaulted one of the youngest of nations to lead all others. Trade has been our protection, but now this nation manufactures a fraction of its capacity, produces little goods, offering only services. Such a short-sighted movement, accompanied by a reluctance to work, has again made this nation as weak as it was when the British dominated this continent.

What I wrote in 1776 concerning the British government:

I challenge the warmest advocate for reconciliation to show a single advantage that this continent can reap by being connected with Great Britain. I repeat the challenge; not a single advantage is derived. Our corn will fetch its price in any market in Europe, and our imported goods must be paid for buy them where we will.

*But the injuries and disadvantages which we sustain by that connection, are without number; and **our duty to mankind at large, as well as to ourselves, instruct us to renounce the alliance**: because, any submission to, or dependence on, Great Britain, tends directly to involve this Continent in European wars and quarrels, and set us at variance with nations who would otherwise seek our friendship, and against whom we have neither anger nor complaint. As Europe is our market for trade, we ought to form no partial connection with any part of it. It is the true interest of America to steer clear of European contentions, which she never can do, while, by her dependence on Britain, she is made the makeweight in the scale of British politics.*

What I see today in the United States government:

I once unsheathed my pen to speak against the enemy of my homeland, the monarchy at my birth. I relocated to this nation in hopes to remove myself from her reach. Unfortunately, the heavy hand of the tyrant stretched across the Atlantic. With pen in hand, I began the push to throw off the harlot. I unsheathe my pen once again, saddened that the enemy no longer resides across the water, but in the capital named after our great general, the father of our country—Washington D.C. There is not a single advantage found in reliance upon this government. The costs are extravagant. The benefits would at first seem few, but I declare the benefits are none. Some will say, if nothing else, we need this government for its army. I dare say the strength of America is not in this government's army, but in this nation's men. General Washington whipped a king's army with the ragtag, ill-equipped, untrained men this nation bore. I am comfortable to rest the defense of this nation against China and Russia upon the arms of the righteous of this nation who have a heart for God and a longing to be free.

President Abraham Lincoln (who came after my death) said something to the nature of, "If destruction be our lot, we must ourselves be its author and finisher." We have seen the greater enemy arise from amongst our own countrymen. These are the people who seemed to be with us, but once in authority, showed they were never part of us. It is as the Apostle John stated concerning the worldly individuals who appeared to be with Christ but were not. He said, "*They went out from us, but they were not of us; for if they had been of us, they would no doubt have continued with us: but they went out, that they might be made manifest that they were not all of us.*" Today, we have a government of lawmakers and administrators who govern as if they were shipped in from a foreign country to rule the citizens of this continent. It is a ruling class separate, out of reach of we the people. It is a tyranny much like what we faced with Great Britain.

What I wrote in 1776 concerning the British government:

*Europe is too thickly planted with Kingdoms to be long at peace, and whenever a war breaks out between England and any foreign power, the trade of America goes to ruin, BECAUSE OF HER CONNECTION WITH BRITAIN. The next war may not turn out like the last, and should it not, the advocates for reconciliation now will be wishing for separation then, because neutrality in that case would be a safer convoy than a man of war. **Every thing that is right or reasonable pleads for separation. The blood of the slain, the weeping voice of nature cries, 'TIS TIME TO PART.***

Even the distance at which the Almighty hath placed England and America is a strong and natural proof that the authority of the one over the other, was never the design of Heaven. The time likewise at which the Continent was discovered, adds weight to the argument, and the manner in which it was peopled, encreases the force of it. The Reformation was preceded by the discovery of America: As if the Almighty graciously meant to open a sanctuary to the persecuted in future years, when home should afford neither friendship nor safety.

What I see today in the United States' government:

In the year 1776, everything reasonable pleaded for separation from Great Britain. The blood of the slain, the weeping voice of nature cried, "Tis time to part." If that were true then, it is truer today. What I am calling for is not a parting from this nation. I am not calling for the writing of a new Constitution. I am calling for the removal of the current governmental officials, of the agencies, of the bureaus, of the blue-ribbon panels, who have grown so complex that they cannot be refined. The blood of the slain infants killed in their mothers' wombs cries that this government must be returned to its original settings. The weeping voice of nature demands that it is time to part from the way in which we are headed. Nature cries, "Men are born men. That cannot be changed." Nature cries, "A woman is born a woman. No surgery can reverse that gender." Nature declares, "Men cannot have children. Men cannot menstruate." Nature is unmoved, "Castrate a bull. He is not made a heifer. Spade the cat. It does not make her a male." The blood of the slain, the weeping voice of nature cries. All nations who once looked upon this nation's government as a beacon, now turn away scoffing. My how the mighty have fallen, they gloat. We, thinking ourselves wise, have become fools.

The discovery of this nation came just before the Reformation. Prior to that historic shift, Christians were refused the right to read God's Word for themselves. They sought to live by its tenets without a religious hierarchy dictating. These took a stand. In their resolve to follow God alone, they were killed, tortured, and evicted from their homes and their homeland. They needed a place to go. God, in His Sovereignty, offered this continent as a shelter for the oppressed Christians. They came here in droves so they could freely pray, worship God, read the Bible, and receive Jesus as Savior. This land became an open Sanctuary—not just a place of safety, but a place of worship, a nation to worship God through His Son Jesus Christ. In such a land, there is freedom. In such a land, there is liberty. In such a land, there is responsibility. In such a land, there is mercy. In such a land, there are laws that men live by, laws enshrined in their hearts, coded on paper. In such a Christian land, there was no persecution of those who disagreed on theology, or even for those who denied there is a God. Have we so soon forgotten?

What I wrote in 1776 concerning the British government:

The authority of Great Britain over this continent, is a form of government, which sooner or later must have an end: And a serious mind can draw no true pleasure by looking forward, under the painful and positive conviction that what he calls "the present constitution" is merely temporary.

What I see today in the United States' government:

The form in which this government is now taking, the movement to an aristocracy cannot last. It will have an end, from internal bankruptcy or external invasion. The Constitution that formed this nation was meant to have an enduring quality. It has met every challenge, until our officials decided to ignore that divinely derived document. Like the spider who destroys her home by cutting the string that holds it in place, we are cutting the string of the Constitution that has secured this nation. Catastrophe is as certain as Sodom's.

What I wrote in 1776 concerning the British government:

As parents, we can have no joy, knowing that this government is not sufficiently lasting to ensure any thing which we may bequeath to posterity: And by a plain method of argument, as we are running the next generation into debt, we ought to do the work of it, otherwise we use them meanly and pitifully. In order to discover the line of our duty rightly, we should take our children in our hand, and fix our station a few years farther into life; that eminence will present a prospect which a few present fears and prejudices conceal from our sight.

What I see today in the United States' government:

I cannot get past the parallels between what Great Britain chained us with and what this current government has repeated. It is plain to see that this government has run into unmanageable debt not just for the next generation, but for the ten generations to follow. Rather than do the difficult work to relieve the debt, the powers-that-be have killed the cow and are picking her bones, rather than let the cow produce offspring and milk for generations to come. Never have I seen such self-immolation. This government has chained enterprise or shipped it to other nations. China prospers, her economy flourishes, her reach extends, all because this nation has decided that every nation should retire at some point and let another rise. All the while, this nation taxes all who will work, spends for those who will not, and prints and borrows money to cover the gap. With any common sense, a person would realize if a family cannot operate this way, how can a collection of families, called a nation, succeed?

If we love our children (and they are our individual children, not the state's), should we not want better for them than we have had? Yet today, it seems, the next generation will fare far worse than the current; the one following even worse than that. Now is the time to do the work to get out of this debt. We are to take our children by the hand. Show them what has been done wrong. Instruct them to do what is right. Fix our station even though there will be suffering involved. Work longer than we intended if that is required. General Washington faced ample reasons to quit. He received many calls to resign. He longed for the fields of Mount Vermon, but he would not quit. He chose to suffer for freedom. The nation and our posterity were at stake. Can the reader of this piece do less?

What I wrote in 1776 concerning the British government:

*Though I would carefully avoid giving unnecessary offence, yet I am inclined to believe, that **all those who espouse the doctrine of reconciliation, may be included within the following descriptions. Interested men, who are not to be trusted, weak men who CANNOT see, prejudiced men who will not see, and a certain set of moderate men who think better of the European world than it deserves; and this***

last class, by an ill-judged deliberation, will be the cause of more calamities to this
Continent than all the other three.

What I see today in the United States' government:

There are many who say let this governmental process continue. Let the Elected continue to exercise their power. Continue to believe that what they are doing is in our best interest, that they know better than the Electors. Those who say such things fall into four categories, as they did in 1776 when I penned this argument. "Those who believe all will be well" consists of those who are interested men but are not to be trusted. They are willing to serve their own interests regardless of the cost to all others.

The second class consists of "those who are weak and cannot see." These will not look beyond the day. They have no thought for tomorrow. They are pleased to eat a fish given than learn how to fish for a lifetime.

The third class are those "prejudiced people who will not see." These have an agenda. They are willing to ignore the consequences of their "cause." They merely want their cause to be accomplished. For example, they seek to cut out fossil fuels, which have been the greatest discovery of the known world. Until fossil fuels and electricity hit the scene, my peers lived much like Jesus and His disciples two thousand years before. But in a mere one hundred years beyond my time, everything changed. These who say, "Cut fossil fuels, stop progress, live as they did in the 1700s," do not realize that the rest of the world will not abide by their fallacy. They are too prejudiced to see that their foolishness will lead to their enslavement to a foreign nation. Those with the cause for climate change, call for the ending of fertilizer. Do they not see that such a move will bring starvation to millions? They are too prejudiced to see.

The absurdity is so thick that they do not see that there is a Creator who knows all that has been, all that is, and all that will be. In His Grand Design, He calibrated the effect of fossil fuels and fertilizers, of cattle and rice production. This earth, a jewel of His Handiwork, can take all that man can dish out. It was not that long ago from this present day that trash was hauled by barge out into the ocean and dumped. The salted seas consumed what was discarded with no lasting effect on the life within it. My generation trusted in the Almighty, in Providence, in God.

We were never once disappointed. Our enemy decided that they would define God in their own image, adjust His Word to fit their fetishes, and they faced the consequences of defeat. Has the reader and his peers not learned what history has taught?

The fourth class are those who believe "this current government and national environment is not as bad as people say." Even more, they say this time is better than it has ever been. This is the worst class of all. In their attempt to end hate speech, they have silenced free speech. They seek to eliminate God with the aim to remove divisions. Do they not see that divisions are starker than ever? To those who say they have ushered in an age of tolerance for the sexually diverse, do they not see the number of suicides rising? For those who say they have brought criminal justice reform, do they not see crime is rampant in every major city? They even placed a murderer who served his time on a parole board. In their enlightenment, they were surprised to see this same man bilk thousands of dollars from COVID funds. For those who say they have corrected the injustices of a racist past, do they not see that they have once again enslaved the minority? For those who say they have fought for reproductive freedom, do they not see the resulting damaged cervix? In the name of reproductive freedom through an oral abortion, do they not see the young girl standing over the toilet, grieving because her dead, floating fetus will not flush for the size? These ill-judged bring more damage upon this generation than the other three, but in harmony they bring an end to a nation that once opened the eyes of an entire world.

What I wrote in 1776 concerning the British government:

It is the good fortune of many to live distant from the scene of present sorrow; the evil is not sufficiently brought to their doors to make them feel the precariousness with which all American property is possessed. But let our imaginations transport us a few moments to Boston; that seat of wretchedness will teach us wisdom, and instruct us for ever to renounce a power in whom we can have no trust. The inhabitants of that unfortunate city who but a few months ago were in ease and affluence, have now no other alternative than to stay and starve, or turn out to beg. Endangered by the fire of their friends if they continue within the city and plundered by the soldiery if they leave it, in their present situation they are prisoners without the hope of redemption, and in a general attack for their relief they would be exposed to the fury of both armies.

What I see today in the United States' government:

It is a blessing to live at a distance from what is going on in this nation. It is easy to rest in the confines of our neighborhoods, shutting the door to the evil that is encroaching. I cannot help but think of Lot, who lived in Sodom for fifteen to twenty years. We read of him stopping the visiting angels from sleeping in the town square. He sought to keep them from being raped by the men of that city. The question comes, how did he know those men were in danger? He had seen many others raped, beaten, and killed in the previous years of residence. I will pass by why he chose to save these two. I would rather question his actions when others were being raped numerous times before. I dare say, he closed his door, spoke louder, played the harp or the lyre, and chose to sing hymns with his family loud enough to drown out the screams just outside his door. That is a blemish to Lot few have considered. In this nation, how many are turning up the music on advanced music makers to ignore the destruction of this country?

Open the doors. Turn off the music. Imagine living in San Franciso, where the homeless reign, where feces fill the streets, where needles are given, and drugs are injected. Consider living in Chicago, where teens gather to destroy whole city blocks, dragging couples from their horseless carriages to beat, rob, and kill. Sit in a school in Tennessee. Watch a catered person kill children merely because they belong to the Christian faith that disagrees with the shooter's lifestyle. Travel with the Executive throughout this nation, from one tragic scene to another. Realize that these things did not happen in my day. The oppressor was not our own citizens, save the Tories. The oppressor was our once-revered government. Is today in 2026 any different? This government has left God. The results are obvious. It is easy to drown out the noise, but at some point, rest assured, they will come for you. I found that to be true in my life in 1776. Time has not diminished the Truth.

What I wrote in 1776 concerning the British government:

Men of passive tempers look somewhat lightly over the offences of Great Britain, *and, still hoping for the best, are apt to call out, "Come, come, we shall be friends* *again for all this."* *But examine the passions and feelings of mankind: bring the doc-* *trine of reconciliation to the touchstone of nature, and then* **tell me whether you can** **hereafter love, honour, and faithfully serve the power that hath carried fire and** **sword into your land?** *If you cannot do all these, then are you only deceiving yourselves,* *and by your delay bringing ruin upon posterity. Your future connection with Britain,* *whom you can neither love nor honour, will be forced and unnatural, and being formed* *only on the plan of present convenience, will in a little time fall into a relapse more* *wretched than the first.* **But if you say, you can still pass the violations over, then I** **ask, hath your house been burnt? Hath your property been destroyed before your** **face? Are your wife and children destitute of a bed to lie on, or bread to live on?** **Have you lost a parent or a child by their hands, and yourself the ruined and** **wretched survivor?** *If you have not, then are you not a judge of those who have.* **But if you have, and can still shake hands with the murderers, then are you un-** **worthy the name of husband, father, friend or lover, and whatever may be your** **rank or title in life, you have the heart of a coward, and the spirit of a sycophant.**

What I see today in the United States' government:

Men of passive tempers today, like 1776, see the offenses of the government and still hope for the best. They assume in the end we will regather as friends. Though President Washington stymied party affiliations, they still existed in the division between Mr. Adams and Mr. Jefferson. Even then, when under attack, they pulled together as one. In the war this nation faced a century or more after my time, again the Democrat and the Republican were of one accord. That was possible because, though the chasm of morals grew, the Biblical ethic remained. It was instilled in our people from childhood forward. The Day of the Lord, Sunday, was reserved for worship, not enterprise. The Bible was the main textbook for our children. Prayer was the thing we did in times of need and in moments of grati-tude. These two, along with fasting, were the major weapons our nation used to drive out the Redcoats. General Washington called for it. Congress proclaimed it. The People gladly joined.

That Spiritual thread was the glue to our national identity. Alexis de Tocqueville witnessed this fact. That cohesive element has been removed. The Lord asks in the Scripture, can two walk together unless they agree? There is a remnant of our nation that still holds to the Truth, but a majority deifies their own desires. What tragedy can pull such opposing views together? Could a terrorist attack? I have read of 9/11. I have studied how quickly this generation came together, and how, with great speed, it divided again. Some of this nation even sided with the attackers. They claimed the terrorists had reason to kill our innocent. General Washington, in a letter written in 1779, asked in the day of trouble, "Where is Mason? Where is Jefferson? Where is Wythe? Where is Nelson?" I ask the same of today's generation. Where is a George Washington, a Patrick Henry, a John Adams, a Nathanael Greene, a Nathan Hale? Where is a Peter Muhlenberg, or a George Whitfield? Where are the pulpits burning with fire, standing on God's Word to declare "Thus says the Lord?" I fear they have all been silenced. Without a return to the foundation of this nation: spiritual, Biblical, Constitutional, sacrificial, I fear my country has reached an inglorious end.

How can the people of this nation continue to have their incomes taken and given to others less worthy? How can the homeowners of this land be forced from their homes because of the burden of taxes? I understand some necessary items are not taxed, like food and water. Is shelter not a necessity? Why is it taxed? On behalf of the poor for whom many are elected claiming to defend, how can they then make it where a poor person cannot retain a home to live in, or one to pass on to their offspring? This nation should never be a nation of the homeless! I hear the echoing pledge that in a few years, people will own nothing and be happy about it. How can that be? It lies at the feet of those who seek to be dependent and those who want to make others their dependents. Children are dying. Kids are being taken from parents. Our basket of freedoms has had its bottom ripped open. Jobs are going overseas. Demands are made for higher wages. Government seconds the motion. Businesses close. Fewer jobs are available. Crime is rampant. Your massive stores are closing because there is no police protection, no punishment for the vandal or the thief. Women are being pulled out of their cars at gunpoint. Men are showering with your little girls. Many have not faced this, so they just turn up the music.

Worse yet, others have faced it. Many have fallen victim. Instead of saying "Enough!" Like the chicken plucked, they have no sense other than to rub up against the one who allows it. If that is you, you are a coward. You have no right to be called husband, father, brother, wife, mother, sister, or friend.

What I wrote in 1776 concerning the British government:

This is not inflaming or exaggerating matters, but trying them by those feelings and affections which nature justifies, and without which, we should be incapable of discharging the social duties of life, or enjoying the felicities of it. *I mean not to exhibit horror for the purpose of provoking revenge, but to awaken us from fatal and unmanly slumbers*, that we may pursue determinately some fixed object. *It is not in the power of Britain or of Europe to conquer America, if she do not conquer herself by delay and timidity.* The present winter is worth an age if rightly employed, but *if lost or neglected, the whole continent will partake of the misfortune; and there is no punishment which that man will not deserve*, be he who, or what, or where he will, that may be the means of sacrificing a season so precious and useful.

What I see today in the United States' government:

It is not the purpose of this writing to exaggerate matters. I am relying upon the feelings that nature justifies. Nature justifies. The created norm is observed in nature. To recreate it or ignore it is a fool's errand. Things that are unnatural can never be made natural. We can call evil good and good evil, but nature shows that such a change in definitions is superficial and fruitless. The ball will not stay suspended in the air. It will come down at some point. The arm will grow tired. The string will break. The pedestal will be knocked over. At some point, the natural overrules.

Nature requires that all men be free. All must awaken from the destructive slumber. This is another complaint I have. It is natural for a male to be superior in some aspect—in strength or in speed. The God of nature has designed that the male is to protect the home, to protect the wife, to protect the children. It is un-natural to believe that a male is better if he is like a female, or for that matter, that a female is better if she becomes like a male. A cow does a poor job becoming a fish. A fish does a poor job trying to fly from tree to tree. It is against all that is right for a male to cower. He is created to stand, to fight, to risk, to stop the aggressor that threatens his home. If men do not return to their designed role, if their duty is neglected, then a whole continent will partake in the misfortune. Whatever punishment comes upon a society that reverses these roles will be well deserved.

What I wrote in 1776 concerning the British government:

It is repugnant to reason, to the universal order of things to all examples from former ages, to suppose, that this continent can longer remain subject to any external power. The most sanguine in Britain does not think so. The utmost stretch of human wisdom cannot, at this time, compass a plan short of separation, which can promise the continent even a year's security. Reconciliation is now a falacious dream. Nature hath deserted the connexion, and Art cannot supply her place. For, as Milton wisely expresses, **"never can true reconcilement grow where wounds of deadly hate have pierced so deep."**

What I see today in the United States' government:

I am very concerned that the hatred once regarded for the British has now become existent between Americans. There is a divide at present that I cannot fathom. The hatred has become deadly. I look at America and I ask myself, "Is this the end?" The Savior said in the Gospel of Matthew that at the end of time, the love of many will grow cold. He also said in the last days, people will be lovers of themselves. This is why there is discord, divorce, and division. There is an order of love. God gave it. Love the Lord thy God will all thy heart, soul, mind, and strength. And love your neighbor as yourself. It was no accident that Jesus gave the order He did. We must love God first. If we love God, we will love each other. If we do not love God. We cannot love each other. It is not possible. It explains how those in power remain aloof to those whom they deem beneath them. The selfish heart beats on, but there is an arrhythmia present.

What I wrote in 1776 concerning the British government:

Every quiet method for peace hath been ineffectual. ***Our prayers have been rejected with disdain; and only tended to convince us, that nothing flatters vanity, or confirms obstinacy in Kings more than repeated petitioning****—and nothing hath contributed more than that very measure to make the Kings of Europe absolute: Witness Denmark and Sweden. Wherefore, since nothing but blows will do, for God's sake, let us come to a final separation, and not leave the next generation to be cutting throats, under the violated unmeaning names of parent and child.*

What I see today in the United States' government:

When I wrote this paragraph, my focus was that the crown and its parliament had rejected our petitions enforced by the prayers to Providence. Now in 2026, I see that prayers are literally rejected with disdain. I have seen news articles after shootings where one side mocks the praying of the other side, intimating that God does not exist at worst, or is powerless at best. Is this where this nation has come—rejecting the Almighty God? If that is the case, then there is no hope for a nation whose government masquerades as a god. Herod Agrippa sought adoration as a god. He was eaten by worms. I see the current unconstitutional government being infiltrated with worms. It cannot hope to live much longer on its current track.

What I wrote in 1776 concerning the British government:

To say, they will never attempt it again is idle and visionary, we thought so at the repeal of the stamp act, yet a year or two undeceived us; as well may we suppose that nations, which have been once defeated, will never renew the quarrel.

As to government matters, it is not in the power of Britain to do this continent justice: The business of it will soon be too weighty, and intricate, to be managed with any tolerable degree of convenience, by a power, so distant from us, and so very ignorant of us; for if they cannot conquer us, they cannot govern us. To be always running three or four thousand miles with a tale or a petition, waiting four or five months for an answer, which when obtained requires five or six more to explain it

in, will in a few years be looked upon as folly and childishness—There was a time
when it was proper, and there is a proper time for it to cease.

What I see today in the United States' government:

One of the reasons we protested taxation without representation was because
the government of Britain did not know us. Their unfamiliarity was because they
allowed us no representatives to acquaint us. There was a distance between the
government and the governed—physical and political. Power was wielded over us
with no opportunity of rebuttal. Today, in this nation, I see the same problem,
only this time the distance cannot be explained by travel of correspondence over
sea. I am in awe of your technology, your ability to communicate in split seconds
with people around the globe or throughout this vast nation, which has been enlarged far beyond what I imagined. One would think with such luxury, the people
could practically push a button. Their representatives would then respond on their
behalf in Washington, D.C.

The fact that Executive and Legislative Branches do not know the people is not
because they cannot, but because they will not. The distance between the working
man in Nebraska and the government man in the Capital is divided by ethics,
morality, and money. One is forced to listen. The other refuses to hear. Emails are
sent. Phone calls are made. Letters are still written. It seems all three are deposited
into a bottomless pit unopened, unread, and unconsidered. What recourse does
the farmer in Nebraska have? He is trying to make a living. He is scurrying to pay
his taxes to keep his land. Those taxes go into the government's pocket to be distributed to the allies of those in office. A portion of that distribution is returned as
campaign donations to keep that special-interest-dependent legislator in power.
The distance with Great Britain was shameful. The distance between the people
and this government is a crime against humanity, a betrayal of all trust, a slap
against all that is good, a mockery of the very people whose vote should matter.

What I wrote in 1776 concerning the British government:

Small islands not capable of protecting themselves, are the proper objects for
kingdoms to take under their care; but there is something very absurd, in supposing

a continent to be perpetually governed by an island. In no instance hath nature made the satellite larger than its primary planet, and as England and America, with respect to each other, reverses the common order of nature, it is evident they belong to different systems: England to Europe, America to itself.

What I see today in the United States' government:

It is amusing to read back over my writing regarding an island ruling a continent. When we defeated that island to win our independence, I never thought I would see the same thing going on in this nation. The small district of Washington, D.C. is ruling the entire continent of the United States of America. What is upsetting is that there is a pocket of appointed agencies, unelected, with no accountability ruling the entire continent. The representatives of the people seem to be on their own little island. They carry on the charade as if they are governing, but excuse what goes on as something out of their hands. The truth is, the only reason professional bureaucrats with staggering salaries, retirement, and health benefits can govern without Congressional action is because Congress approves of their edicts. It is absurd that Americans would let this continue. But then again, most believe things will take care of themselves, never realizing the noose is growing tighter.

What I wrote in 1776 concerning the British government:

I am not induced by motives of pride, party, or resentment to espouse the doctrine of separation and independence; I am clearly, positively, and conscientiously persuaded that it is the true interest of this continent to be so; that every thing short of that is mere patchwork, that it can afford no lasting felicity,—that it is leaving the sword to our children, and shrinking back at a time, when, a little more, a little farther, would have rendered this continent the glory of the earth.

What I see today in the United States' government:

It would be a pleasure to sit with President Washington and reflect upon the effect of those ragtag colonists who simply longed for freedom for their families. I stand amazed at the sixteenth President, Abraham Lincoln. The nation's fight under his watch ended slavery. I have sat for hours with joy contemplating the final fulfillment of my longing to see slavery ended.

The two world wars overwhelm me when I think of how this nation, conceived in liberty, sent its own sons and daughters around the world to save others from despots. We fought tyranny here, and then our offspring fought tyranny for others and won! What a nation we have birthed.

I knew that if our people pushed a little more, a little farther, this continent would be the glory of the earth. I wish I could say it still is. I regret to say, it was. Government has become corrupt. Our people have become enslaved again. The glory of this continent is fading quickly. My return to this century must be to see if I can once again stir the embers of freedom for my people. This generation may have gone too far. This government is complex. It may be that it must be wiped clean. A new start seems to be almost an inevitable notion. The difference between my time and this, at least you have the blueprint. The Constitution lays out the plans for freedom, peace, and happiness if only it will be followed to the letter.

What I wrote in 1776 concerning the British government:

As Britain hath not manifested the least inclination towards a compromise, we may be assured that no terms can be obtained worthy the acceptance of the continent, or any ways equal to the expense of blood and treasure we have been already put to.

*The object, contended for, ought always to bear some just proportion to the expense. The removal of North, or the whole detestable junto, is a matter unworthy the millions we have expended. A temporary stoppage of trade, was an inconvenience, which would have sufficiently balanced the repeal of all the acts complained of, had such repeals been obtained; but if the whole continent must take up arms, if every man must be a soldier, it is scarcely worth our while to fight against a contemptible ministry only. Dearly, dearly, do we pay for the repeal of the acts, if that is all we fight for; for in a just estimation, **it is as great a folly to pay a Bunker-hill price for law, as for land.** As I have always considered the independency of this continent, as an event, which sooner or later must arrive, so from the late rapid progress of the continent to maturity, the event could not be far off. Wherefore, on the breaking out of hostilities, it was not worth the while to have disputed a matter, which time would have finally redressed, unless* *we meant to be in earnest; otherwise, it is like wasting an estate on a suit at law, to regulate the trespasses of a tenant, whose lease is just expiring.* **No man was a warmer wisher for reconciliation than myself, before the fatal nineteenth of April 1775,** *but the moment the event of that day was made known, I rejected the hardened, sullen tempered Pharaoh of England for ever; and disdain the wretch, that with the pretended title of FATHER OF HIS PEOPLE, can unfeelingly hear of their slaughter, and composedly sleep with their blood upon his soul.*

What I see today in the United States' government:

On the nineteenth of April 1775 in Lexington and in Concord, the first shots were fired to defend the ideals of liberty and self-determination. Britain regarded our action as insubordination and treason. I know what follows will be a sensitive subject for the reader. Bear with me. The attack on the United States Capitol on the sixth of January 2021 has been condemned virtually from every side. Let me insert my own opinion. We were right to stand against Great Britain, though even in your day, many believe this was a wrongful act. Generations have been blessed because of what we did. Our actions were against our government at the time— the British government. Many of us came to this continent as citizens of Great Britain, many under the employment or venture of the British crown. We had reaped some benefit from the king and parliament. But when they taxed us beyond measure, when they dictated without consent, when they abused us without one to redress, we had no other option. It was freedom or slavery. We chose freedom at all costs.

On the sixth of January 2021, I cannot reason how that event is viewed so differently from ours. It was against an oppressive government. It was a response to a questionable election. There was no hearing allowed regarding that election. There was no palate for reviewing it. People were forced to accept the outcome given as legitimate. Maybe it was. But when did our government reach the status of never being wrong? The checks-and-balances structure was constructed with the admission that government is run by men. Men are flawed. Thus, the government will err. Government will have corruption. Government, at the least, will make mistakes. Unless man has reached perfection in America over the last two hundred years, then there still needs to be a check on government. That includes a check, or an audit, on elections. The people were not right to storm the Capitol, but they were right to demand investigation. From what I have been told, any call for question on the government is considered a crime against the state. Do you not see? This was what we faced with Great Britain. The king was considered ordained by God. His words were to be reverenced as if they were from God. Now this government that I helped fight for assumes the same mantel. I am sickened to write that, more sickened that it seems to be the case.

What I wrote in 1776 concerning the British government:

But admitting that matters were now made up, what would be the event? I answer, the ruin of the continent. And that for several reasons.

First. The powers of governing still remaining in the hands of the king, he will have a negative over the whole legislation of this continent. **And as he hath shewn himself such an inveterate enemy to liberty, and discovered such a thirst for arbitrary power;** *is he, or is he not, a proper man to say to these colonies, "You shall make no laws but what I please." And is there any inhabitant in America so ignorant, as not to know, that according to what is called the present constitution, that this continent can make no laws but what the king gives it leave to; and is there any man so unwise, as not to see, that (considering what has happened) he will suffer no law to be made here, but such as suit his purpose.* **We may be as effectually enslaved by the want of laws in America, as by submitting to laws made for us in England.** *After matters are made up (as it is called) can there be any doubt, but* **the whole power of the crown will be exerted, to keep this continent as low and humble as possible? Instead of going forward we shall go backward, or be perpetually quarrelling or ridiculously petitioning.—We are already greater than the king wishes us to be, and will he not hereafter endeavour to make us less? To bring the matter to one point. Is the power who is jealous of our prosperity, a proper power to govern us?** *Whoever says No to this question is an independent, for independency means no more, than, whether we shall make our own laws, or, whether the king, the greatest enemy this continent hath, or can have, shall tell us, "there shall be no laws but such as I like."*

What I see today in the United States' government:

The king had power and thirsted for more. This present government has power. It thirsts for arbitrary power. This is clear. I ask the reader this—how many laws have been revoked over the years? Another way to ask this—year by year, are more laws being added or are more laws being removed by this government of America? Each law takes away some freedom. Each law drills down to the more specific, more minute state-of-affairs. Have you not noticed that the government has gone from regulating your wonderful electricity rates, to regulating your electricity source, and now to regulating your electrical appliances? Your lightbulbs are being regulated. Even your toilets are regulated! Your gas stoves are the new target. When will what you wear be delegated? I stand corrected. Clothing is. People wearing shirts deemed impolitic are forced to change. When will what you eat be predetermined? Oh wait, there is already an attack on eating meat and raising cattle.

This nation is not going forward. It is going backward. The script is being flipped from freedom back to slavery. The design of this government at its inception was for the everyday man to leave the plow or the mine or the ministry or the practice to govern for a time, then to return to his or her vocation after impacting the nation for the better. Now, it seems men and women are bred to govern, having never accomplished a thing in private life but to be elected. Those who have never accomplished anything in private enterprise, take from those who have risked and succeeded. The backbone of this nation is being fleeced by those who claim the entrepreneur has gained too much. They say it is not fair. The truth is, every human being has gifts. What they do with those gifts in a free society is their choice. Frugality and industry can make any person in this nation self-sufficient. Only the sluggard cannot succeed in this capitalist society. Sadly, there are sluggards in government getting sluggards money from those who dare to work independent of government intervention and despite government regulation. Should such an incompetent coveter govern? I say no.

What I wrote in 1776 concerning the British government:

But the king you will say has a negative in England; the people there can make no laws without his consent. In point of right and good order, there is something very ridiculous, that a youth of twenty-one (which hath often happened) shall say to several millions of people, older and wiser than himself, I forbid this or that act of yours to be law. But in this place I decline this sort of reply, though I will never cease to expose the absurdity of it, and only answer, that England being the King's residence, and America not so, make quite another case. The king's negative here is ten times more dangerous and fatal than it can be in England, for there he will scarcely refuse his consent to a bill for putting England into as strong a state of defence as possible, and in America he would never suffer such a bill to be passed.

America is only a secondary object in the system of British politics, England consults the good of this country, no farther than it answers her own purpose. Wherefore, her own interest leads her to suppress the growth of ours in every case which doth not promote her advantage, or in the least interferes with it. *A pretty state we should soon be in under such a second-hand government, considering what has happened! Men do not change from enemies to friends by the alteration of a name: And in order to shew that reconciliation now is a dangerous doctrine, I affirm, that it would be policy in the king at this time, to repeal the acts for the sake of reinstating himself in the government of the provinces; in order that **HE MAY ACCOMPLISH BY CRAFT AND SUBTILITY, IN THE LONG RUN, WHAT HE CANNOT DO BY FORCE AND VIOLENCE IN THE SHORT ONE.** Reconciliation and ruin are nearly related.*

What I see today in the United States' government:

Just as British politics consulted the good of the American people only if it benefited the politician, we see those Elected politicians in Washington only doing good if it benefits themselves. Such is the case when an elected official invests in an industry or company prior to passing a law that will benefit that industry or company. Yes, the bill benefited an industry, but was only passed when the politician could personally profit. It irks me that the American people can see such and do nothing. How is it that a person spends millions of dollars for a job that pays thousands? If it were for love of country, I would not object to them, for they would go out poorer than when they went in, leaving the nation and its people richer. This is what I saw in our first government officials. Many lost money to serve. Others would serve, lose money in office, leave their position, make money on their farms, businesses, or law practices, then return to sacrifice more. That is not the state of this government. Men and women spend millions of dollars to win an election to make thousands of dollars in office, and multi-millions more because of that office. They leave richer than when they entered. This cannot be right. It is not good for the nation.

I propose no more spending on campaigns. Let the candidates debate. Have your space-age media cover each. Let the people have access to the discussions and views. Then let them decide on who best to represent them. Let no man or woman make money on the office, or from the office. Put their investments in a blind trust. If an officeholder votes on a bill, no investment by that person can be made where that bill has an impact. At the onset, we had public servants. Today, all I see are public lords. I do not believe the king was worse than what we have today. In fact, the king may be better. At least he would die. Today's government bureaucracy is immortal because the system rules.

Abuses are introduced shrewdly by this government. Actions that take freedom are introduced at first to the public as something that would never be done. They say these are but pondered for academic sake. This relieves the public, except that strategically the matter has been broached. The next time the freedom-stealing idea is presented, the public is familiar with the argument. It is then debated as to the effect such a thing would have. Nothing more. The voting public is again reassured such a thing would never happen. They say it is purely hypothetical. Over time the public's shock is dulled. The matter is tried. Then the matter is expanded. A person wakes up and the matter is enforced. Another freedom falls.

What I wrote in 1776 concerning the British government:

*Secondly. That as even the best terms, which we can expect to obtain, can amount to no more than **a temporary expedient, or a kind of government by guardianship, which can last no longer than till the colonies come of age, so the general face and state of things, in the interim, will be unsettled and unpromising.** Emigrants of* *property will not choose to come to a country whose form of government hangs but by a thread, and who is every day tottering on the brink of commotion and disturbance; and numbers of the present inhabitants would lay hold of the interval, to dispose of their effects, and quit the continent.*

*But the most powerful of all arguments, is, that **nothing but independence, i. e. a continental form of government, can keep the peace of the continent** and preserve it inviolate from civil wars. **I dread the event of a reconciliation with Britain now, as it is more than probable, that it will be followed by a revolt somewhere or other, the consequences of which may be far more fatal than all the malice of Britain.***

What I see today in the United States' government:

Kicking the can down the road is a phrase many have used. The belief that if nothing is done, if no reaction comes from my return of *Common Sense*, there will be peace. Be assured that peace is short-term. A revolt is in the making. An indiscretion can be forgiven. The next one can be ignored. The following one stirs anger. The one beyond that sparks outrage. A final straw will unleash a righteous fury. Lives will be lost, a government toppled. A painful new start will come.

I have lived through that cycle. The longer a thing lies unaddressed, the worse will be the outcome. Mr. Patrick Henry said the time is now to stand while the cost can be contained. Common sense says that abuse unchecked will lead to more. Americans must rise for their freedom. Those in the Elected class who truly do represent the people, who do love freedom, who do fear God, must stand against their nature-offending peers if this nation is to survive.

What I wrote in 1776 concerning the British government:

*Thousands are already ruined by British barbarity; (thousands more will probably suffer the same fate.) Those men have other feelings than us who have nothing suffered. All they now possess is liberty, what they before enjoyed is sacrificed to its service, and having nothing more to lose, they disdain submission. Besides, **the general temper of the colonies, towards a British government, will be like that of a youth, who is nearly out of his time; they will care very little about her. And a government which cannot preserve the peace, is no government at all, and in that case we pay our*** *money for nothing; and pray what is it that Britain can do, whose power will be wholly on paper, should a civil tumult break out the very day after reconciliation? I have heard some men say, many of whom I believe spoke without thinking, that they dreaded an independence, fearing that it would produce civil wars. It is but seldom that our first thoughts are truly correct, and that is the case here; for there are ten times more to dread from a patched up connexion than from independence. I make the sufferers case my own, and I protest, that were I driven from house and home, my property destroyed, and my circumstances ruined, that as a man, sensible of injuries, I could never relish the doctrine of reconciliation, or consider myself bound thereby.*

What I see today in the United States' government:

I wrote in 1776 that a government that cannot preserve the peace is no government at all. I have reviewed your newspapers. I am seeing crime in New York. I am seeing crime in Chicago. I am seeing an autonomous zone in Washington state. I am seeing homeless camps in California. I am seeing stores closing because of theft. I am seeing women trafficked. I am seeing the border overrun. There is no peace. This government you have elected cannot preserve the peace. It seems that this government has no intention to do so. It would rather stand for the chaos. It is not a government at all. I contend it is not an American government because it is not Constitutional.

People fear the overthrow, the change of this government. They are afraid of how they will survive without government healthcare, government retirement, government protection. I can assure the reader that you do not need this government or any government to take care of you. You can work. You can fight. You can save. You can live. You can get care. You can be medically trained.

Many of your neighbors have believed the lie that government is the answer. There were very few things we equipped the federal government to do when we drew up the Constitution revered around the world. It was never the intention at the formation of this nation to make the people wards of the government. This nation was founded for the government to be the servant of the people. That is what is exceptional about this nation. The government was created to literally work for us. That has been flipped on its ear. Today, a large percentage of the American workforce is government-employed. I shudder when I think of the behemoth that has been created.

What I wrote in 1776 concerning the British government:

The colonies have manifested such a spirit of good order and obedience to continental government, as is sufficient to make every reasonable person easy and happy on that head. No man can assign the least pretence for his fears, on any other grounds, that such as are truly childish and ridiculous, viz. that one colony will be striving for superiority over another.

Where there are no distinctions there can be no superiority, perfect equality affords no temptation. The republics of Europe are all (and we may say always) in peace. Holland and Swisserland are without wars, foreign or domestic: **Monarchical governments, it is true, are never long at rest; the crown itself is a temptation to enterprizing ruffians at home; and that degree of pride and insolence ever attendant on regal authority,** swells into a rupture with foreign powers, in instances, where a republican government, by being formed on more natural principles, would negotiate the mistake.

What I see today in the United States' government:

When the people have command of their government, there is peace. When a monarchical or autocratic government rules, it will never be satisfied for long. The power is too tempting. Many want to seize control because with power comes exemptions from the laws passed. A deceived conception of superiority over their fellow man is ignited. This government has become monarchical. There is no peace. Even those in power are vying against each other. They form a fraternity against the Electors. When the challenge has passed, they turn on each other to gain a higher level in the pecking order of regal authority. This is not opinion. History discloses this evil repeatedly.

What I wrote in 1776 concerning the British government:

If there is any true cause of fear respecting independence, it is because no plan is yet laid down. Men do not see their way out—Wherefore, as an opening into that business, I offer the following hints; at the same time modestly affirming, that I have no other opinion of them myself, than that they may be the means of giving rise to something better. Could the straggling thoughts of individuals be collected, they would frequently form materials for wise and able men to improve into useful matter.

Let the assemblies be annual, with a President only. The representation more equal. Their business wholly domestic, and subject to the authority of a Continental Congress.

Let each colony be divided into six, eight, or ten, convenient districts, each district to send a proper number of delegates to Congress, so that each colony send at least thirty. The whole number in Congress will be least 390. Each Congress to sit and to choose a president by the following method. When the delegates are met, let a colony be taken from the whole thirteen colonies by lot, after which, let the whole Congress choose (by ballot) a president from out of the delegates of that province. In the next Congress, let a colony be taken by lot from twelve only, omitting that colony from which the president was taken in the former Congress, and so proceeding on till the whole thirteen shall have had their proper rotation. And in order that nothing may pass into a law but what is satisfactorily just, not less than three fifths of the Congress to be called a majority.—He that will promote discord, under a government so equally formed as this, would have joined Lucifer in his revolt.

What I see today in the United States' government:

I look back at my proposal for a new government to quell fears of what might occur if independence was obtained. I do believe Mr. Madison did a better job in our initial government structure. I was for a unicameral versus my friend Mr. Adams' desire for a bicameral. I believe a bicameral system was advantageous. I spoke of proper rotation. I believe the best rotation at this juncture is a rotation of representatives through term limits. I believe the change of men and women would help this government. More so, a better grade of men and women would solve the nation's ills. In 2026, there is little integrity in office, little fear of God, little fear of judgment, and little fear of consequences.

Again, I am mindful of this push away from what you call fossil fuels. I heard this day that there is an order to make all military equipment electric. That would be fine if the enemies of this nation would do the same. I do not believe the enemies are prone to weaken themselves to join our anemia. If I were China, I would encourage America to move to electric vehicles of war. I would encourage the officials to gather up the guns from the constituency. I would remove the ability of this nation to produce and refine its own oil and gas. If I were Russia, I would give donations to any Elected official who could stop the manufacture of weaponry and ammunition. I would use the excuse of the climate and vow to join in the effort. My words would have evil intent.

If I were an enemy of America, I would send an army of millions across the border disguised as individuals wanting asylum. I would scatter them throughout the nation ready for a coordinated, internal assault. It would be the twenty-first century version of the Trojan Horse. With these efforts, I would get the United States as weak as possible. Its overthrow would be inevitable. I could then seize the ample resources of the American continent which are far beyond my own. Do you not see that if this government that now rules America is not changed, there is an implosion at best, an international takeover at worst? Common sense would dictate that both are likely to occur simultaneously. After the blood and treasure we sacrificed so that this nation could be free, I see the government surrendering while the populace dances to the dirge.

What I wrote in 1776 concerning the British government:

But as there is a peculiar delicacy, from whom, or in what manner, this business must first arise, and as it seems most agreeable and consistent that it should come from some intermediate body between the governed and the governors, that is, between the Congress and the people, let a CONTINENTAL CONFERENCE be held, in the following manner, and for the following purpose.

A committee of twenty-six members of Congress, viz. two for each colony. Two members for each House of Assembly, or Provincial Convention; and five representatives of the people at large, to be chosen in the capital city or town of each province, for, and in behalf of the whole province, by as many qualified voters as shall think proper to attend from all parts of the province for that purpose; or, if more convenient, the representatives may be chosen in two or three of the most populous parts thereof. In this conference, thus assembled, will be united, the two grand principles of business, knowledge and power. The members of Congress, Assemblies, or Conventions, by having had experience in national concerns, will be able and useful counsellors, and the whole, being impowered by the people, will have a truly legal authority.

*The conferring members being met, let their business be to frame a CONTINEN-TAL CHARTER, or Charter of the United Colonies; (answering to what is called the Magna Charta of England) fixing the number and manner of choosing members of Congress, members of Assembly, with their date of sitting, and drawing the line of business and jurisdiction between them: (Always remembering, that **our strength is continental, not provincial:**) **Securing freedom and property to all men, and above all things, the free exercise of religion, according to the dictates of conscience;** with such other matter as is necessary for a charter to contain. Immediately after which, the said Conference to dissolve, and the bodies which shall be chosen comfortable to the said charter, to be the legislators and governors of this continent for the time being: Whose peace and happiness, may God preserve, Amen.*

What I see today in the United States' government:

When I called for a Continental Charter, I had three main tasks in mind—securing freedom, securing property for all men, and above all things, the free exercise of religion. I am grieved to say that all three are being lost in rapid order. Freedoms that we fought for, those that were enumerated in the Bill of Rights, are being modified, ignored, and removed.

Individual property is not secure. The property tax burden makes it virtually impossible for the working men and women to afford their own homes and keep them. After the struggle to set aside a down payment, great deliberation ensues to determine what house a typical family can afford. What is not factored in is the government's ever-increasing tax leech on that house. After an onerous battle, the family will downsize or sell out, being forced to be tenants once again. The stake that an individual can have in this nation is removed. The property tax system has made every American a renter with nothing to pass on to family. This violates the Mosaic law, the Law of God, and everything that is right and good.

The greatest task of our government that I set forth was the freedom of religion. The government that I helped build could not establish a religion nor prohibit the free exercise of one's religion. The problems in America find their root in the elimination of religion, namely the Christian religion. Mr. Adams stated, "Our Constitution was made only for a moral and religious people. It is wholly inadequate to the government of any other." Why does our Constitution seem so ineffective today? Because it is only adequate for a religious and moral people. When the people it oversees become irreligious and immoral, then there is no adherence to it as law, or to any law.

What I see—a coach lost his job in Washington because he knelt to pray on a high school football field. What I see—a baker in Colorado being sued time and again for refusing to make a cake for an event that is against his faith. What I see—the prohibition of prayer at high school graduations. What I see—Thanksgiving becoming a day of sport with no thanks offered to God. What I see—Christmas, the day we chose to celebrate the birth of our Savior, has been stripped of its meaning then renamed the Winter holiday to cement Christ's eviction. What I see - Easter being called Spring recess. What I see—the Bible is not allowed to be read or taught in school.

This nation was founded as a Christian nation. No one was forced to be a Christian. No one was forced to stay a Christian. Today's government has established a religion. It is called humanism. Today's government demands all comply. Today's government has prohibited the free exercise of religion. The result? Crime is rampant. Corruption in government is the norm. We never intended that free exercise of religion to mean in the privacy of one's home. It was intended to guard the individual's right to pray in public, to worship in school, and to have a day of rest on Sunday. This nation and its government are crumbling like a house moved to sit on sand. We made a firm foundation for this nation. It was built on God's Word and the Judeo-Christian faith. Now that it has been moved from that sacred ground, there is nothing sacred at all in the government or in the nation. I grieve. All is crumbling.

What I wrote in 1776 concerning the British government:

Should any body of men be hereafter delegated for this or some similar purpose, I offer them the following extracts from that wise observer on governments Dragon-etti. "The science" says he "of the politician consists in fixing the true point of happiness and freedom. Those men would deserve the gratitude of ages, who should discover a mode of government that contained the greatest sum of individual happiness, with the least national expense."

"Dragonetti on virtue and rewards."

But where says some is the King of America? I'll tell you Friend, he reigns above, and doth not make havoc of mankind like the Royal Brute of Britain. *Yet that we may not appear to be defective even in earthly honors,* **let a day be solemnly set apart for proclaiming the charter; let it be brought forth placed on the divine law, the word of God;** *let a crown be placed thereon, by which the world may know, that so far as we approve as monarchy, that* **in America THE LAW IS KING. For as in absolute governments the King is law, so in free countries the law ought to be King;** *and there ought to be no other. But lest any ill use should afterwards arise, let the crown at the conclusion of the ceremony be demolished, and scattered among the people whose right it is.*

What I see today in the United States' government:

Would that my peers would have joined me for this journey through twenty-first-century America. They would think King George III or his offspring had taken over, transforming the Presidency to Royalty. By the way, we chose the title "President" to infer that this branch position was to merely preside over the affairs of the people. He was never intended to have the authority to dictate through executive order or agency regulations.

Many say that our Founders were not religious, that they did not want God or His mention echoed in government enterprise. How wrong your revisionists are! Our Founders, my friends, would remind all that our only King IS God, the One who reigns above. How tragic that the vast majority in this nation rejects that fact. Until God is seen for who He is, there is little hope for this nation.

I will continue from this complaint. I ordered that there be a Charter established by the representatives of the people and that as a matter of ceremony, that
Charter, the stated law, be placed upon the Divine Law, the Word of God. This
acknowledged that all the laws we deemed necessary had their origin in the Word
of God. That was not a government's establishment of religion, but an acknowl-
edgment that God has established all things.

This is a declaration that God is the King of America. Our laws, based on His,
govern. Another way to say it would be, the law is king here. In monarchies, what
the king says is law. Do you not see this is where this nation is today? What the
government says is law. What the unaccountable Elected say is law. The Electors
have few options to appeal. The law of this land is what is agreed upon by the
Elected. That law exists as a limiting hedge around the governing body. The law
was our defense and safety. Now the laws are manipulated to enslave the Electors.

What I wrote in 1776 concerning the British government:

*A government of our own is our natural right: And when a man seriously reflects
on the precariousness of human affairs, he will become convinced, that it is infinitely
wiser and safer, to form a constitution of our own in a cool deliberate manner, while
we have it in our power, than to trust such an interesting event to time and chance. If
we omit it now, some, Massanello may hereafter arise, who laying hold of popular
disquietudes, may collect together the desperate and discontented, and by assuming
to themselves the powers of government, may sweep away the liberties of the continent like a deluge. Should the government of America return again into the hands of
Britain, the tottering situation of things, will be a temptation for some desperate ad-
venturer to try his fortune; and in such a case, what relief can Britain give? Ere she
could hear the news, the fatal business might be done; and ourselves suffering like the
wretched Britons under the oppression of the Conqueror. Ye that oppose independence
now, ye know not what ye do; ye are opening a door to eternal tyranny, by keeping
vacant the seat of government. There are thousands, and tens of thousands, who would
think it glorious to expel from the continent, that barbarous and hellish power, which
hath stirred up the Indians and Negroes to destroy us, the cruelty hath a double guilt,
it is dealing brutally by us, and treacherously by them.*

What I see today in the United States' government:

It is the natural right of people to have a government of their own, chosen by themselves. A Constitutional republic is the best choice. A nation of laws prevents the greedy, the evil, the desperate, and the discontented from seizing power and eliminating liberties. It also prevents dictators from taking the reins. Each Executive and Congressional member pledges to support and defend the Constitution. Most of our government should be held in contempt or sentenced as perjurers. The state of this nation's affairs shows the cleavage between what is ordered by the Constitution and what is being done.

When the French king was overthrown, the Jacobins placed Robespierre in power. He came from the people, but he was unprincipled. He sought power himself. The French people gave it to him. They thought they had been abused by the king. They quickly found that his abuse was mild compared to the evil man who took his place. If a system of law is not followed, the discontented take power, sweep away liberties like a deluge. Robespierre did just that. He closed theaters because they mocked him. He killed journalists because they questioned him. He removed trials to expedite executing any who opposed him. People quickly seized the opportunity to have people killed over petty grudges, with the charge that they were enemies of the state. The same was done to Jesus by the Pharisees. They had a grudge against Him. They had Him crucified under the pretense that He was an enemy of Rome. Let the France of my day be a lesson to Americans this day. This will be the fate of our nation if the Elected do not return with fealty to the Constitution of the United States.

What I wrote in 1776 concerning the British government:

To talk of friendship with those in whom our reason forbids us to have faith, and our affections wounded through a thousand pores instruct us to detest, is madness and folly. Every day wears out the little remains of kindred between us and them, and can there be any reason to hope, that as the relationship expires, the affection will increase, or that we shall agree better, when we have ten times more and greater concerns to quarrel over than ever?

What I see today in the United States' government:

Reason forbids us to have faith in the government that through a thousand pores instructs us to detest. Every day wears the little remains of kindred between the government that rules and the people who must abide. The more time passes without the Electors taking a stand, the less ability, and resources they will have to make any stand. For many reasons, I am glad that I was not brought up in this present time. Yet, the fire burns within me more than before when I see that what Britain did to us then, we are doing to ourselves now.

What I wrote in 1776 concerning the British government:

Ye that tell us of harmony and reconciliation, **can ye restore to us the time that is past? Can ye give to prostitution its former innocence?** *Neither can ye reconcile Britain and America. The last cord now is broken,* **the people of England are presenting addresses against us. There are injuries which nature cannot forgive; she would cease to be nature if she did. As well can the lover forgive the ravisher of his mistress, as the continent forgive the murders of Britain. The Almighty hath implanted in us these unextinguishable feelings for good and wise purposes. They are the guardians of his image in our hearts. They distinguish us from the herd of common animals.** *The social compact would dissolve, and justice be extirpated from the earth, or have only a casual existence were we callous to the touches of affection. The robber, and the murderer, would often escape unpunished, did not the injuries which our tempers sustain, provoke us into justice.*

O ye that love mankind! Ye that dare oppose, not only the tyranny, but the tyrant, stand forth! Every spot of the old world is overrun with oppression. Freedom hath been hunted round the globe. Asia, and Africa, have long expelled her.—Europe regards her like a stranger, and England hath given her warning to depart. O! receive the fugitive, and prepare in time an asylum for mankind.

What I see today in the United States' government:

The thought that the offenses of this government can be undone should vanish. The government once chosen by us now gathers to attack us. We have been ravaged as have our families. Shall we now forgive the ravager found hiding in the chambers of Congress? Shall we forget the suffering that a detached body of Elected has inflicted? Nature says no. The Almighty still sits enthroned. He still reigns as King, imparting to us unextinguishable knowledge of what is good and wise. We see the opposite in office over us. We were never meant to be herded animals. God made a distinction between us and them. He gave us free will. He created us in His Image. No animal has that identity.

That brings another complaint to mind. This nation now prosecutes those who harm animals. I understand that to a degree. Yet, this same justice is not applied to the infant children in the womb. Many children are left to be preyed upon, seen as sexual outlets for the perverted. To the depths of our souls, we know this is wrong. What is historically and eternally right is labeled wrong in this nation. What is historically and immutably wrong is now called right.

O ye that love mankind! Stand forth. Throughout history, the governments of this earth have outlawed freedom. Yet, every soul hungered for it. This nation alone was able to put freedom where it belonged. Are we to throw off that freedom to join the dregs of nations past? Are you willing to see the freest nation on earth destroyed?

Of the Present Ability of America
with Miscellaneous Reflections

What I wrote in 1776 concerning the British government:

I HAVE never met with a man, either in England or America, who hath not confessed his opinion, that a separation between the countries would take place one time or other: And there is no instance in which we have shown less judgment, than in endeavoring to describe, what we call, the ripeness or fitness of the continent for independence.

As all men allow the measure, and vary only in their opinion of the time, let us, in order to remove mistakes, take a general survey of things, and endeavor if possible to find out the VERY time. But I need not go far, the inquiry ceases at once, for the TIME HATH FOUND US. The general concurrence, the glorious union of all things, proves the fact.

What I see today in the United States' government:

If there is a need for the government to cease to be the lord of the people (and there is), the question to be handled is when? The government has successfully made its residents dependent. Many believe that to break away, there must be a weaning off period. Sadly, such a weaning is delayed by the lord who does not want it to end, and the servant who fears what will happen to them afterward. It is like when a parent has an adult child who has never left home. The parent enjoys the company and control. The child enjoys the provision. Nature shows that though each may not want the break, each needs the break. It is unnatural for a child to live with the parent their entire life. They never realize self-dependence or self-determination. They are stunted by their own will, fear, or laziness. And at some point, the parent dies. What then? Even the birds push their young out of

the nests. With dependence upon the government, freedoms are taken, self-determination is lost. Government grows. The individual declines. In 1776, the time
to break from Britain was then.

For 2026, the time to break from government lordship is now. Government
must be decreased immediately. Government handouts must be minimized at
once. Self-dependence by every citizen of this nation must be owned. The result
will be a healthy government. Individuals will have more because the government
leech has been removed. At the current rate of things, financial collapse is on the
horizon. When that occurs, what will the dependents do then? The whole nation
is at stake. Now is the time to break the dependence upon the American government, as we broke our dependence on the British one.

What I wrote in 1776 concerning the British government:

*'Tis not in numbers but in unity that our great strength lies: yet our present
numbers are sufficient to repel the force of all the world. The Continent hath at
this time the largest body of armed and disciplined men of any power under
Heaven: and is just arrived at that pitch of strength, in which no single colony is
able to support itself, and the whole, when united, is able to do any thing. Our
land force is more than sufficient, and as to Naval affairs, we cannot be insensible that
Britain would never suffer an American man of war to be built, while the Continent
remained in her hands. Wherefore, we should be no forwarder an hundred years hence
in that branch than we are now; but the truth is, we should be less so, because the
timber of the Country is every day diminishing, and that which will remain at last,
will be far off or difficult to procure.*

What I see today in the United States' government:

In 1776, there was an urgency. The enemy had taken up arms against us. At
that time, I had to bolster the confidence of our populace that our strength was
derived from our unity. I look at the foreign adversaries that threaten America
today in 2026. Our chief weakness is that we are not unified. Politics and selfish
gain have rendered this nation the Divided States of America.

You have a game called football. On a screen one night, I saw what is called a draft. Organizations draft young men to play on their teams. Thousands of spectators with an allegiance to a particular team gathered. They all had a favorite to whom they supported, but together, their chief allegiance was to a pastime, a sport. I watched it on the television set. I have to say it is quite remarkable to my eighteenth-century mind that I could be in my home in New Rochelle watching something occurring in Missouri (a state that joined with great conflict years after I left this earth, per Ms. Tanswell).

I was grieved that there was no reference to the flag of the United States, no banners showing a love for this nation, no prayer to God in Heaven to bless the gathering. What hurt me beyond this, I fear our people have become more in love with a sport than a nation. You have become dull to the dangers your enemies pose. They can soon take away all that you have and then your life. This is the consequence of a government that has left the Constitution, an Elected group whose self-serving actions have alienated them from what truly matters.

As to national defense, in 1776, I wrote that our Continent has the largest body of armed and disciplined men. Today, I hear alarms sounding over the access to guns, that guns should be taken from the hands of the citizens. The unelected agencies of this nation are requiring a record of who owns firearms, how many, and what kind. Can you not see this is more than a census exercise? Does anyone read history in this era? Britain sought to take our guns, too. This is what sparked the "shot heard round the world." If a government can take the guns of its citizens, then the citizens have no way to hold that government at bay. This is why Mr. Madison penned the Second Amendment. Mr. Jefferson agreed. What Thomas Jefferson wrote in wisdom is a matter I wholeheartedly concur: "Whenever any form of government becomes destructive of these ends (life, liberty, and the pursuit of happiness), it is the right of the people to alter or abolish it, and to institute new government." Our form of government is ideal. It is not the Constitutional government that needs to be changed, but those who are operating at its head. Guns in the homes are what slowed the British government from entry. Guns may be your last resort against this one, too.

That is a look at the internal. On the external, your enemies of this day encourage the United States government to take your guns. In this way, there will be fewer obstacles should they advance to take the whole continent. Guns and discipline are needed by the men and women of this nation. United and armed, there is nothing this nation cannot do. There is no attack this nation cannot quell. America's greatest defense is the ability to move offensively against any aggressor. Have you not learned?

What I wrote in 1776 concerning the British government:

Were the Continent crowded with inhabitants, her sufferings under the present circumstances would be intolerable. The more seaport-towns we had, the more should we have both to defend and to lose. Our present numbers are so happily proportioned to our wants, that no man need be idle. The diminution of trade affords an army, and the necessities of an army create a new trade.

*Debts we have none: and whatever we may contract on this account will serve as a glorious memento of our virtue. Can we but leave posterity with a settled form of government, an independent constitution of its own, the purchase at any price will be cheap. But to expend millions for the sake of getting a few vile acts repealed, and routing the present ministry only, is unworthy the charge, and is **using posterity with the utmost cruelty; because it is leaving them the great work to do, and a debt upon their backs from which they derive no advantage. Such a thought's unworthy a man of honour, and is the true characteristic of a narrow heart and a piddling politician.***

What I see today in the United States' government:

The rulers of this nation are doing horrendous damage to future generations. As parents of succeeding generations, we must do the work to fix the government abuses and erase the national debt. There is a need to reform this government in our day so that our children will not have to do so in theirs. The noose is tight now. Can we imagine how it will be for our children if we do not make the effort to correct it now? Who longs for their children to be enslaved? By doing nothing, we bring that dread into a future reality. Put this government back in its place.

This nation sought to follow the Holy Scriptures at the onset—to not be a borrower of any nation. Granted, in the American Revolution, we did become debtors to France, but over time that was remedied. The debt this nation has incurred in 2026 is beyond my mathematical mind to fathom. If this nation allows its government to continue to borrow and print money, our children will be shackled, even impoverished, by what the parents have done. It will be up to the kids to drag that burden from which they received no benefit. Anyone willing to pass unmanageable debt along to the next generation is not honorable, not worthy to be a citizen of this nation or a parent in this nation. Bring spending within the confines of minimal taxation, setting aside an amount each year to reduce the debt.

What I wrote in 1776 concerning the British government:

The debt we may contract doth not deserve our regard if the work be but accomplished. No nation ought to be without a debt. A national debt is a national bond; and when it bears no interest, is in no case a grievance. Britain is oppressed with a debt of upwards of one hundred and forty millions sterling, for which she pays upwards of four millions interest. And as a compensation for her debt, she has a large navy; America is without a debt, and without a navy; yet for the twentieth part of the English national debt, could have a navy as large again. The navy of England is not worth at this time more than three millions and a half sterling.

What I see today in the United States' government:

In the war, I was for the debt if it would accomplish liberty. I saw the need for America to have a military and a naval force. Regrettably, the debt of America today has little to do with its national defense. It has much to do with its dereliction of sound stewardship tied to vast greed. There is a national bond that we all should count as our debt—a debt to freedom, a debt to those who have suffered before, a debt to those who will follow. The first responsibility of government, the main reason for debt, is to keep its citizens safe from enemies foreign and domestic.

What I wrote in 1776 concerning the British government:

The first and second editions of this pamphlet were published without the following calculations, which are now given as a proof that the above estimation of the navy is a just one. See Entic's "Naval History," Intro., p. 56.

The charge of building a ship of each rate, and furnishing her with masts, yards, sails, and rigging, together with a proportion of eight months boatswain's and carpenter's sea-stores, as calculated by Mr. Burchett, Secretary to the navy.

For a ship of 100 guns, ... 35,553 £
90 " 29,886
80 " 23,638
70 " 17,785
60 " 14,197
50 " 10,606
40 " 7,558
30 " 5,846
20 " 3,710

And hence it is easy to sum up the value, or cost, rather, of the whole British navy, which, in the year 1757, when it was at its greatest glory, consisted of the following ships and guns.

Ships	Guns	Cost of One	Cost of All
6	100	35,553 £	213,318 £
12	90	29,886	358,632
12	80	23,638	283,656
43	70	17,785	764,755
35	60	14,197	496,895
40	50	10,605	424,240
45	40	7,558	340,110
58	20	3,710	215,180

85 sloops, bombs, and fireships,

one with another at 2,000 ... 170,000
Cost, ... 3,266,786 £
Remains for guns, ... 233,214
Total, ... 3,500,000 £

No country on the globe is so happily situated, or so internally capable of raising a fleet as America. Tar, timber, iron, and cordage are her natural produce. We need go abroad for nothing. Whereas the Dutch, who make large profits by hiring out their ships of war to the Spaniards and Portuguese, are obliged to import most of the materials they use. We ought to view the building a fleet as an article of commerce, it being the natural manufactory of this country. 'Tis the best money we can lay out. A navy when finished is worth more than it cost: And is that nice point in national policy, in which commerce and protection are united. Let us build; if we want them not, we can sell; and by that means replace our paper currency with ready gold and silver.

What I see today in the United States' government:

When I walked this earth the first time, I could honestly say that no country on the globe was so happily situated and capable of raising a fleet as America. Two hundred and fifty years later, I can attest that my statement is still true. So where lies the problem? America seems to have no interest in manufacturing. This government and nation willingly farms out the business of production to others—namely the Asian countries.

The Dutch were the shipbuilders of my day. They made their fortunes from others' inability to produce. This nation has the ability and the resources to produce, but either is too lazy or simply disinclined to invest in its own defense. There seems to be a belief that if America stops its manufacture of weaponry, lays down what it has, then the world will do the same. That is contrary to all common sense. If America lays down its ability to make war, the enemies will gladly enter with little loss.

I challenge all who read this. Get back to building the fleet. China has surpassed us in naval strength. Russia has surpassed us in hypersonic technology. America has even sold its uranium holdings to an enemy. I come to one of two conclusions, neither good. Either the American government wishes our destruction, or they are deluded by some utopian view. The greatest challenge to America's existence is not Climate Change, but the enemies abroad who care nothing for the climate. It is proven not by their words, but by their deeds.

I am caught by my last sentence from those years past. Build ships. Use what we need, sell the rest to our allies. Exchange paper money for ready gold and silver. Inflation has hit the U.S. Dollar. It is on the verge of collapse. When the gold standard was abandoned, the printing of money became unhinged. The dollar is now heading to a worthless state. Nations around the world are divesting from the dollar. What does this government do? Print more! No!!! Return the tie between the dollar and precious metal. It is the only check to the Elected's malfeasance. It is the only guarantor of value. General Washington faced this lunacy in America's first real war. It has been revived sevenfold in this current age.

What I wrote in 1776 concerning the British government:

In point of manning a fleet, people in general run into great errors; it is not necessary that one-fourth part should be sailors. The Terrible privateer, captain Death, stood the hottest engagement of any ship last war, yet had not twenty sailors on board, though her complement of men was upwards of two hundred. A few able and social sailors will soon instruct a sufficient number of active landsmen in the common work of a ship. Wherefore we never can be more capable of beginning on maritime matters than now, while our timber is standing, our fisheries blocked up, and our sailors and shipwrights out of employ. Men of war, of seventy and eighty guns, were built forty years ago in New England, and why not the same now? Ship building is America's greatest pride, and in which she will, in time, excel the whole world. The great empires of the east are mainly inland, and consequently excluded from the possibility of rivalling her. Africa is in a state of barbarism; and no power in Europe hath either such an extent of coast, or such an internal supply of materials. Where nature hath given the one, she hath withheld the other; to America only hath she been liberal to both. The vast empire of Russia is almost shut out from the sea; wherefore her boundless forests, her tar, iron and cordage are only articles of commerce.

What I see today in the United States' government:

Shipbuilding is also necessary for trade. There must be ships for war, ships for transport, and ships for escort. They are necessary for peace and battle. Whatever America undertakes in unity, she can outdistance any nation in the world. There was a time when America was number one in naval power. We have resigned from that position to our detriment. Look how the Almighty has blessed this nation. Some in Europe have coastlines but no materials. Others have materials but no coast. God has given America both liberally. The strengths of America should not be shuttered to the dependence on others.

This bounty of the American continent applies to all types of fuel as well. America has the natural resources to power its own needs domestically for homes and transportation, as well as for military purposes. Why would this nation surrender that advantage. It is one thing to be captured and made a slave. It is another thing to bow one's head, extend one's arms, and submit to having every freedom removed. America is at that point today. My peers in 1776 would be aghast. If I were to return to them at this moment and relay to them the future state of their nation, they would call me a fool and have me returned to a French prison.

What I wrote in 1776 concerning the British government:

In point of safety, ought we to be without a fleet? We are not the little people now which we were sixty years ago; at that time we might have trusted our property in the streets, or fields rather, and slept securely without locks or bolts to our doors and windows. The case is now altered, and our methods of defence ought to improve with our increase of property. A common pirate, twelve months ago, might have come up the Delaware, and laid the city of Philadelphia under contribution for what sum he pleased; and the same might have happened to other places. Nay, any daring fellow, in a brig of fourteen or sixteen guns, might have robbed the whole Continent, and carried off half a million of money. These are circumstances which demand our attention, and point out the necessity of naval protection.

What I see today in the United States' government:

The weak state of America regarding its defense was aptly stated in my initial correspondence of *Common Sense*. The state of America today has decayed to that condition again. Some report that America would not have ammunition to engage in a war for more than two weeks at the present. Other than the miraculous Six-Day War in Israel, I have never heard of a war lasting less than a few weeks. General Washington had to become an expert in retreat, for he was constantly out of weaponry, ammunition, and men. He had the wilderness, the wisdom, and God's Hand to succeed. The ability to retreat at this time has been removed. Build up now before it is too late.

One other addendum to this excerpt. There have been times in America when a person could trust their property to the streets, sleep in their unlocked homes, but those days of righteousness have passed. When there was a fear of God, there was a control on our actions. With no fear of God, more law enforcement is required. In this nation right now, there is little fear of God. There is also a reduction in law enforcement. The result: it is Sodom on our streets. Nothing is safe. No one is safe—not the child, not the elderly. No one is safe. Common sense would require our direction be reversed. This is just the word of an old man from long ago who once had the ear of his nation.

What I wrote in 1776 concerning the British government:

Some perhaps will say, that after we have made it up with Britain, she will protect us. Can they be so unwise as to mean that she will keep a navy in our harbors for that purpose? Common sense will tell us that the power which hath endeavoured to subdue us, is of all others the most improper to defend us. Conquest may be effected under the pretence of friendship; and ourselves, after a long and brave resistance, be at last cheated into slavery. And if her ships are not to be admitted into our harbours, I would ask, how is she going to protect us? A navy three or four thousand miles off can be of little use, and on sudden emergencies, none at all. Wherefore if we must hereafter protect ourselves, why not do it for ourselves? Why do it for another?

What I see today in the United States' government:

The men and women in the current government have done everything in their power to subdue the people under them. Land is taken under the guise of the public good. Children are being taken under the name of safety to allow sex change operations, which are preposterous, a sin against nature, a denial of reality, bringing sterility to a generation. People are allowed to construct tents on the city sidewalks, declaring it their homestead. Prayer is disallowed under the false interpretation of separation of church and state. Medical licenses are being revoked for any doctor who dares to disagree with the government regarding pandemic protocols. Common sense says such a government should not be trusted at all to defend us. They have not in every other matter, what makes us think they will in some other?

What I wrote in 1776 concerning the British government:

The English list of ships of war is long and formidable, but not a tenth part of them are at any time fit for service, numbers of them are not in being; yet their names are pompously continued in the list; if only a plank be left of the ship; and not a fifth part of such as are fit for service can be spared on any one station at one time. The East and West Indies, Mediterranean, Africa, and other parts, over which Britain extends her claim, make large demands upon her navy. From a mixture of prejudice and inattention we have contracted a false notion respecting the navy of England, and have talked as if we should have the whole of it to encounter at once, and for that reason supposed that we must have one as large; which not being instantly practicable, has been made use of by a set of disguised Tories to discourage our beginning thereon. Nothing can be further from truth than this; for if America had only a twentieth part of the naval force of Britain, she would be by far an overmatch for her; because, as we neither have, nor claim any foreign dominion, our whole force would be employed on our own coast, where we should, in the long run, have two to one the advantage of those who had three or four thousand miles to sail over before they could attack us, and the same distance to return in order to refit and recruit. And although Britain, by her fleet, hath a check over our trade to Europe, we have as large a one over her trade to the West Indies, which, by laying in the neighborhood of the Continent, lies entirely at its mercy.

What I see today in the United States' government:

The British government overextended its reach. Had any with a built-up navy challenged her, Britain would not have stood. Resting in her decaying inventory, The British took comfort in the number of its ships, not the seaworthiness of her fleet. This is the state of America's military force. We have been lulled by our stockpile over the enemies. Since the enemies have encroached our numbers with military might of their own, America, deluded, now boasts in her quality of defense. Just like Britain, the United States force has a decaying military, spending money on concepts rather than hardware.

This United States' government has extended itself too thin. Instead of focusing on the few matters where government is needed, she has inserted herself in matters she knows nothing about – business, education, production, and energy to name a few. This current government has little to no expertise in any of these matters but demands to be over all of them. The result – chaos, inefficiency, and an unnatural impediment. The worst consequence of all is the current inability to defend her people from enemies abroad who are stirring for a fight.

What I wrote in 1776 concerning the British government:

Some method might be fallen on to keep up a naval force in time of peace, if we should judge it necessary to support a constant navy. If premiums were to be given to merchants to build and employ in their service ships mounted with twenty, thirty, forty, or fifty guns (the premiums to be in proportion to the loss of bulk to the merchant), fifty or sixty of those ships, with a few guardships on constant duty, would keep up a sufficient navy, and that without burdening ourselves with the evil so loudly complained of in England, of suffering their fleet in time of peace to lie rotting in the docks. To unite the sinews of commerce and defence is sound policy; for when our strength and our riches play into each other's hand, we need fear no external enemy.

In almost every article of defence we abound. Hemp flourishes even to rankness so that we need not want cordage. Our iron is superior to that of other countries. Our small arms equal to any in the world. Cannon we can cast at pleasure. Saltpetre and gunpowder we are every day producing. Our knowledge is hourly improving. Resolution is our inherent character, and courage hath never yet forsaken

us. Wherefore, what is it that we want? Why is it that we hesitate? From Britain we can expect nothing but ruin. If she is once admitted to the government of America again, this Continent will not be worth living in. Jealousies will be always arising; insurrections will be constantly happening; and who will go forth to quell them? Who will venture his life to reduce his own countrymen to a foreign obedience? The difference between Pennsylvania and Connecticut, respecting some unlocated lands, shows the insignificance of a British government, and fully proves that nothing but Continental authority can regulate Continental matters.

What I see today in the United States' government:

Our nation, during the crisis of British oppression, had everything we needed to defend ourselves. To go with the resources, we had the inherent character of resolve to overcome. We also had the courage to right all our mistakes. In this current day, the resolve has dampened, the courage has diminished to cowardice. If the government that now rules this continent is not corrected, this nation will not be worth living in. We have all the tangibles we need to remain the strongest nation on the globe. We lack the intangibles that had been our greatest strength.

What I wrote in 1776 concerning the British government:

Another reason why the present time is preferable to all others is, that the fewer our numbers are, the more land there is yet unoccupied, which, instead of being lavished by the king on his worthless dependents, may be hereafter applied, not only to the discharge of the present debt, but to the constant support of government. No nation under Heaven hath such an advantage as this.

What I see today in the United States' government:

There was a day in this nation, that land to our west extended far and wide. There was a joy to realize that each could dream of owning land, living under their own vine and fig tree. Today, yearning to own a home and land has dissipated. I personally do not understand that. Regardless of where the reader stands on such possessions, is it a concern to know that rather than the British king taking the land and lavishing it on his friends, this government of America now owns almost thirty percent of all land, making inroads to gain more? They claim it is to preserve it, to keep it for us, the citizens. When did this American government become the warden of its people? When did we allow government to own for itself what rightfully belongs to the people? Need I remind you, this is a government of the people, for the people, and by the people—not separate from the people.

I propose the government-held land be kept at a minimum, only as military purposes and active national parks warrant. Beyond that, the land should be returned to the citizens through purchase with the money going to pay down the national debt. This will reduce government overreach. It will also reduce the burden of taxation upon its citizens. This will increase the viability of this nation, reestablishing its credibility on the world stage.

What I wrote in 1776 concerning the British government:

The infant state of the Colonies, as it is called, so far from being against, is an argument in favour of independence. We are sufficiently numerous, and were we more so we might be less united. **'Tis a matter worthy of observation that the more a country is peopled, the smaller their armies are. In military numbers, the ancients far exceeded the moderns; and the reason is evident, for trade being the consequence of population, men became too much absorbed thereby to attend to anything else. Commerce diminishes the spirit both of patriotism and military defence.** *And history sufficiently informs us that the bravest achievements were always accomplished in the non-age of a nation.* **With the increase of commerce England hath lost its spirit.** *The city of London, notwithstanding its numbers, submits to continued insults with the patience of a coward.* **The more men have to lose, the less willing are they to venture. The rich are in general slaves to fear, and submit to courtly power with the trembling duplicity of a spaniel.**

What I see today in the United States' government:

Never did I claim to be a prophet. Any who read what I wrote long ago, would think that I had some innate gift of prophecy. That has never been the case. I am a student of history. With history, one can accurately foresee the future. King Solomon said there is nothing new under the sun. This is true. The more a nation grows, the more it gets involved in commerce, ease, and wealth. With the mind absorbed in commerce, the less apt it is to concern itself with matters of survival. It forgets the dangers that once threatened its existence. The dangers still exist, but they are far removed from the psyche. Commerce diminishes the spirit of patriotism and military defense. Money has a way of brainwashing its holders. Everyone does what is right in their own eyes. They have no worries about what form of government rules so long as they believe their personal life will continue in ease. For money, basketball stars will accept shoe deals with China, the enemy of their nation, the oppressor of millions.

It is why Silas Deane profited from this nation's fight for Independence. So long as his nest was feathered, it mattered not to him the outcome of the war or his countrymen. It is the spirit of Deane that I see pervasive in the leadership of this nation. Men and women elected by their peers arrive in Washington, D.C., cut deals, accept speaking fees, and are awarded board positions with financial reward from enemies who seek the defeat of our nation. So long as their nest is feathered, it matters not to them the outcome of this nation or its people. What the Elector and the Elected alike miss, if the tree of this nation falls, there is a high probability their padded nests will go too.

What I wrote in 1776 concerning the British government:

Youth is the seed-time of good habits as well in nations as in individuals. It might be difficult, if not impossible, to form the Continent into one government half a century hence. The vast variety of interests, occasioned by an increase of trade and population, would create confusion. Colony would be against colony. Each being able would scorn each other's assistance; and while the proud and foolish gloried in their little distinctions **the wise would lament that the union had not been formed before. Wherefore the present time is the true time for establishing it. The intimacy which is contracted in infancy, and the friendship which is formed in misfortune, are of all others the most lasting and unalterable.** *Our present union is marked with both these characters; we are young, and we have been distressed; but our concord hath withstood our troubles, and fixes a memorable era for posterity to glory in.*

What I see today in the United States' government:

Now is the time to pull together to change the direction of this nation. We can be unified if for no other reason than misfortune. We each find ourselves victims, in one way or another, of this present government. The approval ratings of the Executive and the Legislative Branches are at all-time lows. It is against common sense that officials can continue to be elected time and again if the ratings are that poor across the board. There are only two explanations for this.

One, the voters in each district believe their representative is not the one at fault, but blame lies with representatives of the others. To counter this, I ask the Elector to review the voting record of their representative to realize it is not theirs that is good. Theirs has joined in evil with the others.

Two, the system by which elections are executed has numerous intended defects. Today, the rulers say it is un-American to question the outcome of an election. In my day, it was fully American, yea patriotic, to question everything. It is why we, the people, took back our government. We made it our own. Will you not do the same?

What I wrote in 1776 concerning the British government:

The present time, likewise, is that peculiar time which never happens to a nation but once, viz., the time of forming itself into a government. Most nations have let slip the opportunity, and by that means have been compelled to receive laws from their conquerors, instead of making laws for themselves. First, they had a king, and then a form of government; whereas the articles or charter of government should be formed first, and men delegated to execute them afterwards; but from the errors of other nations let us learn wisdom, and lay hold of the present opportunity—TO BEGIN GOVERNMENT AT THE RIGHT END.

When William the Conqueror subdued England, he gave them law at the point of the sword; and, until we consent that the seat of government in America be legally and authoritatively occupied, we shall be in danger of having it filled by some fortunate ruffian, who may treat us in the same manner, and then, where will be our freedom? Where our property?

What I see today in the United States' government:

Most nations had dictators or kings take control. He or she then laid down the law. In this nation, we established the law. We then appointed leaders to comply with that law. Today, that law has been circumvented by the leaders. They have become the law unto themselves. Day by day, session after session, they lay down more laws upon us. Most of those laws come from executive agencies, committees, and bureaus. This is governing from the wrong end. The result—we are losing our liberties. We are losing our property. "You will own nothing and be happy" is their precept. This pamphlet is not a call to overthrow our form of government but to elect officials who will once again be governed by us and the law. We must get government back to the format where the Law governs the Elected.

What I wrote in 1776 concerning the British government:

As to religion, I hold it to be the indispensable duty of government to protect all conscientious professors thereof, and I know of no other business which government hath to do therewith. Let a man throw aside that narrowness of soul, that selfishness of principle, which the niggards of all professions are so unwilling to part with, and he will be at once delivered of his fears on that head. Suspicion is the companion of mean souls, and the bane of all good society. **For myself, I fully and conscientiously believe that it is the will of the Almighty that there should be a diversity of religious opinions among us. It affords a larger field for our Christian kindness; were we all of one way of thinking, our religious dispositions would want matter for probation; and on this liberal principle I look on the various denominations among us to be like children of the same family, differing only in what is called their Christian names.**

What I see today in the United States' government:

I have spent much space writing about God, the Bible, and religion. I contend that the freedoms we enjoy began with the one freedom of religion. In 1776, our great concern was that this nation be free to worship, not free from worship. We were free to worship God, not forbidden to worship Him. We formed a Christian nation. I make no apologies for that. As a Christian nation, we realized that no one should be forced to come to Christ. We knew that God loved all. Our hope was that our Christian kindness would lead people to want the same. Our greatest concern was not Christianity being imposed, but a denomination of Christianity being favored over another. Let this fact be rediscovered, etched in stone, never to be defaced again.

What I wrote in 1776 concerning the British government:

In page [97] I threw out a few thoughts on the propriety of a Continental Charter (for I only presume to offer hints, not plans) and in this place I take the liberty of re-mentioning the subject, by observing that **a charter is to be understood as a bond of solemn obligation, which the whole enters into, to support the right of every separate part, whether of religion, professional freedom, or property. A firm bargain and a right reckoning make long friends.**

What I see today in the United States' government:

Our Constitution was an agreed-upon, solemn obligation, a contract between the people and their government to be honored for all time, protecting the freedoms thereby stated. The Tenth Amendment was written to reaffirm this: "The powers not delegated to the United States by the Constitution, nor prohibited by it to the States, are reserved to the States respectively, or the people." The people are to have the vast amount of power, not the government. It is to our shame that such a statement is imperceivable.

What I wrote in 1776 concerning the British government:

I have heretofore likewise mentioned the necessity of a large and equal representation; and there is no political matter which more deserves our attention. A small number of electors, or a small number of representatives, are equally danger-ous. But if the number of the representatives be not only small, but unequal, the danger is increased. As an instance of this, I mention the following: **when the petition of the associators was before the House of Assembly of Pennsylvania, twenty-eight members only were present; all the Bucks county members, being eight, voted against it,** *and had seven of the Chester members done the same, this whole province had been governed by two counties only; and this danger it is always exposed to. The unwarrantable stretch likewise, which that house made in their last sitting, to gain an undue authority over the delegates of that province, ought to warn the people at large how they trust power out of their own hands.* A set of instructions for their delegates were put together, which in point of sense and business would have dishonoured a school-boy, and after being approved by a few, a very few, without doors, were carried into the house, and there passed IN BEHALF OF THE WHOLE COLONY; whereas, did the whole colony know with what ill will that house had entered on some necessary public measures, they would not hesitate a moment to think them unworthy of such a trust.

What I see today in the United States' government:

This nation formed a governmental body with the intent to have many Electors with many representatives dispersed for their cause. When few vote, wrong can easily govern all. When few represent, a small body can make demands on the masses. The tail should not wag the dog. The island should not govern the continent. We have thrust the power from our own hands onto the Elected few.

What I see in this nation today, the voters or Electors see little impact their votes make. Their votes do not put the desired official in office. Those in office rule against the people's wishes. The cost to object is prohibitive. The potential penalty is severe. This was what it was like to live under the king of England. This is what it is like again in the United States of America. United, we can object with impact. Apart and inactive, we are slaves.

What I wrote in 1776 concerning the British government:

Immediate necessity makes many things convenient, which if continued would grow into oppressions. Expedience and right are different things. *When the calamities of America required a consultation, there was no method so ready, or at that time so proper, as to appoint persons from the several houses of assembly for that purpose; and the wisdom with which they have proceeded hath preserved this Continent*

from ruin. But as it is more than probable that we shall never be without a CON-
GRESS, every well wisher to good order must own that the mode for choosing
members of that body deserves consideration. And I put it as a question to those who
make a study of mankind, whether representation and election is not too great a power
*for one and the same body of men to possess? **When we are planning for posterity, we***
ought to remember that virtue is not hereditary.

It is from our enemies that we often gain excellent maxims, and are frequently sur-
prised into reason by their mistakes. Mr. Cornwall (one of the Lords of the Treasury)
treated the petition of the New York Assembly with contempt, because THAT house,
he said, consisted but of twenty-six members, which trifling number, he argued, could
not with decency be put for the whole. We thank him for his involuntary honesty.

What I see today in the United States' government:

It is convenient to ignore the abuses of the current Elected bodies. It is best to
be inconvenienced now, then oppressed further. There is a political philosophy
that has permeated your day—"Never let a crisis go to waste." I saw the same in
1776. When an immediate necessity occurs, it is convenient to let the authorities
take whatever action necessary to meet the emergency. Citizen beware! Those infringements on liberty that we allow for the moment will soon dissolve into oppression. Do not be so quick as to look to the government for a solution. Work it
out among yourselves. You are Americans. You are able on your own.

To rid this nation of office holders who take advantage of crisis to grow their
power, resolve to consider every candidate before voting. The current system is to
vote for the one who has the most money, who can spin his or her message in the
marketplace, putting a face so deceptive that ancient Greek actors would be envi-
ous. Today, people vote for the mask, where beneath is a scoundrel opposite the
one displayed. Again, I propose this nation move away from a monetized campaign, and return to one of public debate with media coverage. Let every voter see
and hear for themselves what the candidate says. Vote according to what is virtuous. By the way, virtue is not something one passes on any more than a saving
faith.

One additional caveat that I believe should be added to the laws of this nation.
If an elected official does not do what he or she says that person should be tried

for contempt by the Electors. If they are found to have lied on any issue, promise, or stand, they should immediately be removed from office. How can we be free if we have a government that lies to we the people? Should not the leader be as honest as the public if not more? The Word of God requires a higher accountability for those in leadership.

What I wrote in 1776 concerning the British government:

*To CONCLUDE, however strange it may appear to some, or however unwilling they may be to think so, matters not, but **many strong and striking reasons may be given to show that nothing can settle our affairs so expeditiously as an open and determined declaration for independence.***

What I see today in the United States' government:

I am calling for independence from the government. Let this government's role be returned to its original intent. Let business run freely. Let individuals live their lives in their best interest, cautiously watching that they do to others what they would have them do unto them. Let each person, let each business operate with self-responsibility. There should be no bailouts of business by the taxpayer through their government. There should be no reward for not working, nor compensation for those who did not frugally save. The masses of America will make better, informed decisions if left to themselves. The nation will be stronger for it.

What I wrote in 1776 concerning the British government:

First. — It is the custom of Nations, when any two are at war, for some other powers, not engaged in the quarrel, to step in as mediators, and bring about the preliminaries of a peace; But while America calls herself the subject of Great Britain, no power, however well disposed she may be, can offer her mediation. Wherefore, in our present state we may quarrel on for ever.

Secondly. — It is unreasonable to suppose that France or Spain will give us any kind of assistance, if we mean only to make use of that assistance for the purpose of

repairing the breach, and strengthening the connection between Britain and America;
because, those powers would be sufferers by the consequences.

Thirdly. — **While we profess ourselves the subjects of Britain, we must, in the**
eyes of foreign nations, be considered as Rebels. The precedent is somewhat danger-
ous to their peace, for men to be in arms under the name of subjects; we, on the
spot, can solve the paradox; *but to unite resistance and subjection requires an idea*
much too refined for common understanding.

What I see today in the United States' government:

We cannot pledge subjection to a government body that refuses to be subject
to the law we gave. We cannot be dependent on the government while claiming
independence from the government. The government truly is dependent upon the
people. It produces nothing to sustain itself. We provide the money for the governmental salaries. They, in turn, take those salaries we funded to imprison us, the
benefactors.

What I wrote in 1776 concerning the British government:

Fourthly. — *Were a manifesto to be published, and despatched to foreign Courts,*
setting forth the miseries we have endured, and the peaceful methods which we have
ineffectually used for redress; declaring at the same time that not being able longer to
live happily or safely under the cruel disposition of the British Court, we had been
driven to the necessity of breaking off all connections with her; at the same time, assur-
ing all such Courts of our peaceable disposition towards them, and of our desire of
entering into trade with them; such a memorial would produce more good effects to this
Continent than if a ship were freighted with petitions to Britain.

Under our present denomination of British subjects, we can neither be received nor
heard abroad; the custom of all Courts is against us, and will be so, until by an inde-
pendence we take rank with other nations.

These proceedings may at first seem strange and difficult, but like all other steps
which we have already passed over, will in a little time become familiar and agreeable;
and **until an independence is declared, the Continent will feel itself like a man**

who continues putting off some unpleasant business from day to day, yet knows it must be done, hates to set about it, wishes it over, and is continually haunted with the thoughts of its necessity.

What I see today in the United States' government:

This last sentence that I wrote well sums up the expediency by which we must act. This government cannot continue to grow in power, increase its bottomless debt, weaken its defenses, open its borders, and hope long to survive. Though we would rather put off fixing this for another day, we know it must be done. We do not want to set about what it will take to do it. We hate the thought of what it will take. We are haunted by the consideration, but together we must act from necessity immediately—for ourselves and our posterity. One does not wait to quench a fire until it spreads throughout the home. One acts at the first sight of flame if there is any hope of preserving what has been built.

Appendix

What I wrote in 1776 concerning the British government:

*SINCE the publication of the first edition of this pamphlet, or rather, on the same day on which it came out, the **king's speech** made its appearance in this city. Had the spirit of prophecy directed the birth of this production, it could not have brought it forth at a more seasonable juncture, or at a more necessary time. The bloody-mindedness of the one, shows the necessity of pursuing the doctrine of the other. Men read by way of revenge. And the speech, instead of terrifying, prepared a way for the manly principles of independence.*

Ceremony, and even silence, from whatever motives they may arise, have a hurtful tendency when they give the least degree of countenance to base and wicked performances, wherefore, if this maxim be admitted, it naturally follows, that the king's speech, IS being a piece of finished villany, deserved and still deserves, a general execration, both by the Congress and the people.

*Yet, as the domestic tranquillity of a nation, depends greatly on the chastity of what might properly be called NATIONAL MANNERS, it is often better to pass some things over in silent disdain, than to make use of such new methods of dislike, as might introduce the least innovation on that guardian of our peace and safety. And, perhaps, it is chiefly owing to this prudent delicacy, that the king's speech hath not before now suffered a public execution. **The speech, if it may be called one, is nothing better than a wilful audacious libel against the truth, the common good, and the existence of mankind; and is a formal and pompous method of offering up human sacrifices to the pride of tyrants.***

*But this general massacre of mankind, is one of the privileges and the certain consequences of kings, for as nature knows them not, they know not her, and **although they are beings of our own creating, they know not us, and are become the gods of their creators**. The speech hath one good quality, which is, that it is not calculated to deceive, neither can we, even if we would, be deceived by it. Brutality and tyranny appear on* *the face of it. It leaves us at no loss: And every line convinces, even in the moment of reading, that he who hunts the woods for prey, the naked and untutored Indian, is less savage than the king of Britain. Sir John Dalrymple, the putative father of a whining jesuitical piece, fallaciously called, "The address of the people of England to the inhabitants of America," hath perhaps from a vain supposition that the people here were to be frightened at the pomp and description of a king, given (though very unwisely on his part) the real character of the present one: "But," says this writer, "if you are inclined to pay compliments to an administration, which we do not complain of (meaning the Marquis of Rockingham's at the repeal of the Stamp Act) it is very unfair in you to withhold them from that prince, by whose NOD ALONE they were permitted to do any thing." This is toryism with a witness! Here is idolatry even without a mask: And* **he who can calmly hear and digest such doctrine, hath forfeited his claim to rationality an apostate from the order of manhood and ought to be considered as one who hath not only given up the proper dignity of man, but sunk himself beneath the rank of animals, and contemptibly crawls through the world like a worm.**

What I see today in the United States' government:

I call upon the reader to use the technology that you have been blessed to develop. Listen skeptically to what your leaders in office tell you. Their words are a libel against the truth as much as King George's were. They tell us things that we know, if even considered for a second, to be vastly irrational. They tell us that the southern border is secure. The video images show thousands crossing every day. Cities are overrun by illegal aliens. Yet, the officials declare what is seen is not seen. Some of your leaders have said that they must pass a law before they can read it. Really? They make laws that consist of thousands of pages, and are voted on a day later, when no human has the capacity to read and comprehend what is written in that amount of time.

Will you not ask the questions necessary? Who wrote these bills? How long did it take them to write such long novels, soon to be enshrined as laws? Often, bills are passed without letting the public even have access to review them. The excuse that is given—national security prevents sharing. That sounds acceptable, but is everything now a national security issue? Who defines what falls into that category?

The representatives who answer to the people are there for our good. We, in theory, should be able to trust them. But, as long as the same representatives are in place, election after election beyond any explanation, can we have any confidence our interests and freedoms are being defended?

What I wrote in 1776 concerning the British government:

However, it matters very little now what the king of England either says or does; he hath wickedly broken through every moral and human obligation, trampled nature and conscience beneath his feet, and by a steady and constitutional spirit of insolence and cruelty procured for himself an universal hatred. It is now the interest of America to provide for herself. She hath already a large and young family, whom it is more her duty to take care of, than to be granting away her property to support a power who is become a reproach to the names of men and christians, whose office it is to watch the morals of a nation, of whatsoever sect or denomination ye are of, as well as ye who are more immediately the guardians of the public liberty, if ye wish to preserve your native country uncontaminated by European corruption, ye must in secret wish a separation. But leaving the moral part to private reflection, I shall chiefly confine my further remarks to the following heads:

What I see today in the United States' government:

Just as the king had wickedly broken through every moral and human obligation, trampled nature and conscience with insolence and cruelty, drawing the hatred of the day, this current government has done the same. I declare they have done worse than the king. We had no say in what king would rule over us. He inherited his position. His allegiance, to a degree, was reserved for his family. But this government has been chosen by the people of this nation. The agencies, councils, and bureaus were created by them. They have willfully abused our trust for their own gain. I say those who govern us today are the greater offenders.

You ask me, Mr. Paine, what solution do you propose to this? I believe we must take back this government. Perhaps the people of this nation will declare "Enough!" And those in office with any virtue at all will join the cry of the nation. Perhaps the radical reform is to cast out all who are currently in office with a fresh election of new men and women. Put all agencies on a sunset term. Let those newly elected decide which ones should stay and which ones should be abolished. Those in office could hold their place until their replacements are chosen. They then could give limited guidance in the requested areas.

A more feasible solution is two-fold. Let there be term limits for every elected official. And let the elected officials work from their districts, not on the "island" in the District of Columbia. This would give the Electors, the constituents, the greatest influence. It would also become a very costly proposition for lobbyists needing to be at five hundred and thirty-five places at once. Technology of today makes working from one's district manageable. It will reduce the cost to the people. It will increase the access and power of the voters. Trips to Washington should be minimal. Again, the bureaucracy of agencies must be cut down dramatically. A government of the people, by the people, and for the people can be restored.

You ask, why would anyone in office surrender their prestige at the Capitol? And regarding term-limits, why would anyone willingly give up their position after a few years? My answer to the question is simple—they love their nation and their nation's people more than themselves. I am writing this as a man who made no money from my initial *Common Sense*. I donated every proceed to the war effort in my day. I took up arms to fight for my nation. I willingly suffered. Nathan Hale stated that he regretted he had but one life to give for his country. We would find very quickly who loves this nation. The scoundrel in office for their own benefit would quickly object, thus be easily detected. It is not uncommon for a government to be thrown out with another one taking its place. We threw the king out of this nation. We were the better for it. I contend the same can be done today. This nation will be better for it. Let the office holder return to the servanthood of the people. I believe serving in Congress should be like serving on jury duty. It is necessary as a good citizen. It is also a sacrifice that each willingly makes for a period of time. After serving, the citizen returns to their families and vocations to live under the laws they passed. This is what serving in government should emulate. Removing an ever-growing dictating monstrosity will cause every family to thrive.

What I wrote in 1776 concerning the British government:

First, That it is the interest of America to be separated from Britain.

Secondly, Which is the easiest and most practicable plan, RECONCILIATION or INDEPENDENCE? with some occasional remarks.

In support of the first, I could, if I judged it proper, produce the opinion of some of the ablest and most experienced men on this continent: and whose sentiments on that head, are not yet publicly known. **It is in reality a self-evident position: for no nation in a state of foreign dependence, limited in its commerce, and cramped and fettered in its legislative powers, can ever arrive at any material eminence. America doth not yet know what opulence is; and although the progress which she hath made stands unparalleled in the history of other nations, it is but childhood compared with what she would be capable of arriving at, had she, as she ought to have, the legislative powers in her own hands.** *England is at this time proudly coveting what would do her no good were she to accomplish it; and the continent hesitating on a matter which will be her final ruin if neglected.* **It is the commerce and not the conquest of America by which England is to be benefited, and that would in a great measure continue, were the countries as independent of each other** *as France and Spain; because the specious errors of those who speak without reflecting. And among the many which I have heard, the following seems the most general, viz. that had this rupture happened forty or fifty years hence, instead of now, the continent would have been more able to have shaken off the dependence. To which I reply, that our military ability, at this time, arises from the experience gained in the last war, and which in forty or fifty years' time, would be totally extinct. The continent would not, by that time, have a quitrent reserved thereon will always lessen, and in time will wholly support, the yearly expense of government. It matters not how long the debt is in paying, so that the lands when sold be applied to the discharge of it, and for the execution of which the Congress for the time being will be the continental trustees.*

What I see today in the United States' government:

America's people, in their state of dependence upon the government, have not experienced the bounty of their individual efforts. Though we are the richest people in the world, we could be better off still if we find the courage to throw off the chains of this government.

Here is an interesting outcome to consider. Not only would the people be better off, so would the government. If the American people could function freely, they would be better off financially. The people's increased wealth would provide the government with more resources to carry on its limited Constitutional duties. Tying down the ingenuity of the people produces less revenue, reduces the tax base, grows the impoverished, requiring higher taxes and more welfare, leading to the unending cycle of self-destruction. The ultimate result is tyranny, a condition not foreign to us now.

What I wrote in 1776 concerning the British government:

I proceed now to the second head, viz. Which is the easiest and most practicable plan, reconciliation or independence; with some occasional remarks.

He who takes nature for his guide, is not easily beaten out of his argument, and on that ground, I answer generally that independence being a single simple line, contained within ourselves; and reconciliation, a matter exceedingly perplexed and complicated, and in which a treacherous capricious court is to interfere, gives the answer without a doubt.

The present state of America is truly alarming to every man who is capable of reflection. Without law, without government, without any other mode of power than what is founded on, and granted by, courtesy. Held together by an unexampled occurrence of sentiment, which is nevertheless subject to change, and which every secret enemy is endeavoring to dissolve. Our present condition is, Legislation without law; wisdom without a plan; a constitution without a name; and, what is strangely astonishing, perfect independence contending for dependence. The instance is without a precedent, the case never existed before, and who can tell what may be the event? The property of no man is secure in the present un-braced system of things. The mind of the multitude is left at random, and seeing no fixed object before them, they pursue such as fancy or opinion presents. Nothing is criminal; there is no such thing as treason, wherefore, every one thinks himself at liberty to act as he pleases. The Tories would not have dared to assemble offensively, had they known that their lives, by that act, were forfeited to the laws of the state. A line of distinction should be drawn between English soldiers taken in battle, and inhabitants of America taken in arms. The first are prisoners, but the latter traitors. The one forfeits his liberty, the other his head.

Notwithstanding our wisdom, there is a visible feebleness in some of our proceedings which gives encouragement to dissensions. The continental belt is too loosely buckled: And if something is not done in time, it will be too late to do any thing, and we shall fall into a state, in which neither reconciliation nor independence will be practicable. **The king and his worthless adherents are got at their old game of dividing the continent, and there are not wanting among us printers who will be busy in spreading specious falsehoods. The artful and hypocritical letter which appeared a few months ago in two of the New York papers, and likewise in two others, is an evidence that there are men who want both judgment and honesty.**

What I see today in the United States' government:

I cannot help but take this excerpt to address the freedom of the press. It was our intention that the press be a check on the government. It was the king's desire to shut down any press that would not adhere to his rule or his messaging. Robespierre endeavored the same. In times past, we saw the press closed, the writers imprisoned. I faced these threats myself. The parties that rule call any report that contradicts them as spreading lies.

In 2026, the government lauds media outlets for their biased reporting. The authorities use media outlets as their voice. What has alarmed me in this day is how media exalts others in media for their bias. The press members interview others of their ilk to craft the news. The government rewards such. It also uses its agencies to harass non-compliers. I have even seen the previous Executive of this nation giving out the questions that the media can ask, silencing those who question the Executive's motives.

Our First Amendment stated, "Congress shall make no law…abridging the freedom of speech, or of the press, or the right of the people to peaceably assemble, and to petition the Government for a redress of grievances." Speech in your day is muted if it is considered hurtful to others. The Founders placed no limits on the freedom of speech. Hurtful speech provokes thought. Thought provoked can right an incorrect opinion or strengthen a correct one. It is in debate that we learn. It is in open discussion that we communicate. It was the contest between two political adversaries, Lincoln and Douglas, that united them as friends.

Back to the press. The press is to be that fourth check on the government. The minute they unite, the people are the unsuspecting victims. The press is to report wrongs by the government. I sought to do this. Mr. Franklin did as well. At one point, we were both in government. Yet, we both viewed the press as a necessary critic. How much better is society when those in office must prove they are doing what is in the best interest of the people? When they are not, the press is to make such public so that it can be redressed, or the person removed.

What I wrote in 1776 concerning the British government:

*It is easy getting into holes and corners, and talking of reconciliation: But do such men seriously consider how difficult the task is, and how dangerous it may prove, should the continent divide thereon? Do they take within their view all the various orders of men whose situation and circumstances, as well as their own, are to be considered therein? **Do they put themselves in the place of the sufferer whose all is already gone, and of the soldier, who hath quitted all for the defence of his country?** If their ill-judged moderation be suited to their own private situations only, regardless of others, the event will convince them that "they are reckoning without their host."*

What I see today in the United States' government:

Some will choose to live and let live. Others will, for the sake of their office, try to plaster over what is already broken. Before one assumes the position of idleness, consider those who have lost their homes to this government, their freedoms for speaking out, their businesses for not acquiescing, or their elected offices for standing up. One may think those examples do not affect you. Know this; at some point, they will come for you, too.

What I wrote in 1776 concerning the British government:

Put us, say some, on the footing we were in the year 1763: To which I answer, the request is not now in the power of Britain to comply with, neither will she propose it; but if it were, and even should be granted, I ask, as a reasonable question, By what means is such a corrupt and faithless court to be kept to its engagements? Another parliament, nay, even the present, may hereafter repeal the obligation, on the pretence of its being violently obtained, or not wisely granted; and, in that case, Where is our redress? No going to law with nations; cannon are the barristers of crowns; and the sword, not of justice, but of war, decides the suit. To be on the footing of 1763, **it is not sufficient, that the laws only be put in the same state, but, that our circumstances likewise be put in the same state; our burnt and destroyed towns repaired or built up, our private losses made good, our public debts (contracted for defence) discharged; otherwise we shall be millions worse than we were at that enviable period.** *Such a request, had it been complied with a year ago, would have won the heart and soul of the continent, but now it is too late. "The Rubicon is passed." Besides, the taking up arms, merely to enforce the repeal of a pecuniary law, seems as unwarrantable by the divine law, and as repugnant to human feelings, as the taking up arms to enforce obedience thereto. The object, on either side, doth not justify the means; for the lives of men are too valuable to be cast away on such trifles. It is the violence which is done and threatened to our persons; the destruction of our property by an armed force; the invasion of our country by fire and sword, which conscientiously qualifies the use of arms: and the instant in which such mode of defence became necessary, all subjection to Britain ought to have ceased; and the independence of America should have been considered as dating its era from, and published by, the first musket that was fired against her. This line is a line of consistency; neither drawn by caprice, nor extended by ambition; but produced by a chain of events, of which the colonies were not the authors.*

I shall conclude these remarks, with the following timely and well-intended hints. **We ought to reflect, that there are three different ways by which an independency may hereafter be effected, and that one of those three, will, one day or other, be the fate of America, viz. By the legal voice of the people in Congress; by a military power, or by a mob:** *It may not always happen that our soldiers are citizens, and the multitude a body of reasonable men; virtue, as I have already remarked, is not hereditary, neither is it perpetual.* **Should an independency be brought about by the first** *of those means, we have every opportunity and every encouragement before us, to form the noblest, purest constitution on the face of the earth. We have it in our power to begin the world over again. A situation, similar to the present, hath not happened since the days of Noah until now.*

What I see today in the United States' government:

As we sought to extricate ourselves from the chains of Great Britain, three options came to mind: by the legal voice of the people in Congress, by a military power, or by a mob. Today in America, you face the same options. By a new start in Congress, the government can return to the noblest, purest Constitution on the face of the earth. You have it in your power, as we did in our day, to begin this nation over again. Noah and his family were able to start afresh when wickedness was washed from control. This should be our method.

Otherwise, an oppressive government can use its military to force the people into submission. Once upon a time, our military was comprised of our citizens. There may come a point where it, like the press, becomes the tenacles of the government. My fear is also that if things are not corrected soon, an outside military will have the ability to put this nation under their authoritarian rule, which will be worse than the first.

Mob rule is the last alternative. We are seeing evidence of that throughout the nation. Mob actions are allowed under the label "justified." There are cries that this nation is a democracy. What are they teaching in these schools? This is not a democracy. It is a Constitutional Republic with the very aim of eliminating mob rule. When the mob rules, no government can exist but the strongest ruffian. We saw that with the Jacobins and Robespierre. When the mob rules, the hurting are squashed, as are the weak. No. Let the change be through our Congress, through a new start of that Congress.

What I wrote in 1776 concerning the British government:

The birthday of a new world is at hand, and a race of men, perhaps as numerous as all Europe contains, are to receive their portion of freedom from the events of a few months. The reflection is awful, and in this point of view, how trifling, how ridiculous, do the little paltry cavilings of a few weak or interested men appear, when weighed against the business of a world.

Should we neglect the present favorable and inviting period, and independence be hereafter effected by any other means, we must charge the consequence to ourselves, or to those rather whose narrow and prejudiced souls are habitually opposing the measure, without either inquiring or reflecting. There are reasons to be given in support of independence which men should rather privately think of, than be publicly told of. **We ought not now to be debating whether we shall be independent or not, but anxious to accomplish it on a firm, secure, and honorable basis, and uneasy rather that it is not yet began upon. Every day convinces us of its necessity.** *Even the Tories (if such beings yet remain among us) should, of all men, be the most solicitous to promote it; for as the appointment of committees at first protected them from popular rage, so, a wise and well established form of government will be the only certain means of continuing it securely to them. Wherefore, if they have not virtue enough to be WHIGS, they ought to have prudence enough to wish for independence.*

In short, independence is the only bond that tie and keep us together. We shall then see our object, and our ears will be legally shut against the schemes of an intriguing, as well as cruel, enemy. We shall then, too, be on a proper footing to treat with Britain; for there is reason to conclude, that the pride of that court will be less hurt by treating with the American States for terms of peace, than with those, whom she denominates "rebellious subjects," for terms of accommodation. It is our delaying in that, encourages her to hope for conquest, and our backwardness tends only to prolong the war. *As we have, without any good effect therefrom, withheld our trade to obtain a redress of our grievances, let us now try the alternative, by independently redressing them ourselves, and then offering to open the trade. The mercantile and reasonable part of England, will be still with us; because, peace, with trade, is preferable to war without it. And if this offer be not accepted, other courts may be applied to.*

What I see today in the United States' government:

It will not be through begging that the present rulers will oblige our requests. They must see the people as on equal footing as they themselves. But more, they must see that they are to be the servants. Until we take back this government, until we ensure honest elections, until we take a stand, all freedoms are subject to be taken and then given back as favors. China has this process in place. Its citizens are free to travel if they are in good standing with the monarchical regime. All businesses are regulated on that ground as well. Freedoms there are granted by the government. Freedoms have been justly proclaimed here in the United States as coming from God. Those rights are unalienable and are not to be taken or given.

We, the people, must take a stand against our own government. We must demand they submit to us. Only then can the authorities in power see the people as not just equals. They will see the truth. The citizens are the ones from whom they find their employment. May that employment be temporary for each. This will provide better representation.

What I wrote in 1776 concerning the British government:

On these grounds I rest the matter. And as no offer hath yet been made to refute the doctrine contained in the former editions of this pamphlet, it is a negative proof, that either the doctrine cannot be refuted, or, that the party in favor of it are too numerous to be opposed. WHEREFORE, instead of gazing at each other with suspicious or doubtful curiosity, let each of us hold out to his neighbor the hearty hand of friendship, and unite in drawing a line, which, like an act of oblivion, shall bury in forgetfulness every former dissension. Let the names of Whig and Tory be extinct; and let none other be heard among us, than those of a good citizen, an open and resolute friend, and a virtuous supporter of the RIGHTS of MANKIND, and of the FREE AND INDEPENDENT STATES OF AMERICA.

What I see today in the United States' government:

Let the Divided States of America unite. Let this nation's citizens no longer be called Democrats, Independents, Libertarians, Greens, Republicans, or by any other name. Let us be Americans supporting the rights of mankind within the free, independent states of America. Let us be united by one heart for the God who made us, owing to Him alone the title of King and Sovereign. Let common sense again govern. The Hippocratic Oath of a physician should apply to any who seeks to serve in government – do no harm. More specifically stated, the rule for all who seek to serve should be, "Do not do anything that will destroy this nation, its families, its enterprise, its freedoms, or its individuals. Defend life, liberty, and the pursuit of happiness". Follow the Constitution with all fidelity.

I just heard my name called. I must return from whence I came. I have to say, it has been quite an eye-opening experience being back in this nation that I have loved. I want the reader to know that I am greatly disappointed in what I have seen. I have always been hopeful about the heart that beats within an American. I pray to see it revived. I will be watching. What will you do?

HISTRIA

BOOKS

HISTRIA
PERSPECTIVES

BOOKS THAT CHALLENGE AND ENLIGHTEN

FOR THESE AND OTHER GREAT BOOKS VISIT
HISTRIABOOKS.COM